Modern youngsters still enjoy the carousel.
(Jayne Horsburgh)

Kirkcaldy Links Market

Carol McNeill

Fife Council – Community Services
2004

Published by
Fife Council – Community Services

Printed by
Cordfall Ltd
0141 572 0878

Contents

Youngsters look longingly at the sweet stalls set up in Links Street around 1890, wondering what to spend their Victorian pennies on.
(Fife Council Libraries)

Crowds flock to the 1905 Market on Sands Road, with mothers and babies dressed in their best for the occasion.
(Fife Council Libraries)

Chapter One
Early Days

Kirkcaldy Links Market has a special atmosphere of its own: a heady mixture of fun, sophistication and nostalgia made up of bright lights, music, breath-taking rides and colourful sideshows, all adding up to the longest street fair in Europe and the largest in Scotland. Life in the Lang Toun changes for ten days in April when the Market lorries roll in.

Generations of local people have been going down to the Prom to enjoy the spectacle which they remember from their childhood and now take their children and grandchildren to see. Generations of the same families of show people have been providing the entertainment in what is not just their business, but a way of life. And although almost everything else has changed down the passage of the centuries, the traditional Links Market weather with that raw east wind has surely been around for as long as the Market itself.

The mixture of tradition and innovation which is today's Links Market has gradually evolved from a charter granted by King Edward I in 1304, when a yearly fair was allowed to be held in Easter week, to last for three days. The first fair was held a year later, and from these simple origins has grown the six-day annual event which has become part of the fabric of Kirkcaldy.

The main function of the original markets was to sell the necessities of life, which in the fourteenth century were pretty basic. This was, after all, only a few years before Bannockburn, three hundred years before the Union of the Crowns and four hundred years before Scotland's first Parliament went into abeyance. Farmers brought their eggs, vegetables, meat and grain; fishermen had shellfish and mackerel on the stalls; tradesmen such as cobblers, coopers, basket-makers and tinsmiths were kept busy; and dealers in everything from pottery to rolls of cloth displayed their wares. Even then the crowds looked for some entertainment, and jugglers, acrobats, street musicians and singers travelled round the country to provide it.

As the years rolled down, the concept of selling goods at the Market continued and then extended to sideshows, entertainments and rides. Linktown of Abbotshall had been a separate Burgh of Barony since the seventeenth century, and even before its amalgamation with Kirkcaldy in 1876, stalls were sited in the widest part of the Links at Market Square at the foot of Pottery Wynd (now Methven Road). The side shows and other fairground attractions were on the Sands Road, which before it was transformed into the Esplanade in 1923 was a long, narrow and unmetalled road bounded by a rubbish dump, and known at the time as 'Kirkcaldy's disgrace.' When the tramways came to Links Street around 1902, the two sites amalgamated along the length of the Prom, where—despite various attempts on different occasions to re-site it—it still operates every year.

In the 1840s, it was the Linktown Police Commission which collected site rents or dues, and stamped their initials on all the stands with a branding iron. In 1850 the Commissioners fixed the rental charges, with large caravans at 1/6 each, small caravans at a shilling, and stands from threepence to a shilling, according to their size. In the first indication that the Market was no longer confined to Links Street, they also ordered that the large caravans were to be sent to "the Braes at the foot of the lanes", referring to the Seabraes or Sands Road at the end of the many wynds leading off the Links. This would leave "12 feet to be kept quite clear in the centre of the street in all time coming" for trades and stands. In 1877, according to Kirkcaldy Town Council Minutes, the site of the Market was determined as Links Street (between Bell Wynd and Watery Wynd) and Sands Road between Bell Wynd and Pottery Wynd.

During the 1850s, the Market was a one-day event on the third Friday in April, but even then there were sideshows and entertainments to supplement the traders' stalls. One of the earliest newspaper reports of the Market, in the *Fifeshire Advertiser* of 1852, refers not only to stalls selling shoes, household utensils, and confectionery but also to "shows of every sort and degree, from the bawbee peep and famous roundabout up to fair specimens of drama and

Wilmot's Caledonian Hunters are pictured in 1914 with the Helter-skelter in the background.
(Fife Council Libraries)

A horse-drawn roundabout, Smith's Pony Circus, drew the crowds around 1900. One of the carousel horses can be made out on the right of the picture.
(Fife Council Museums: Kirkcaldy Museum and Art Gallery)

farce and magnificent collections of wild beasts". Boots and shoes, baskets, and barrels—all basics of everyday life—were on sale along with dolls, cradles and wheelbarrows for children. Sideshows included the diorama of the Russian war, a performing pony, wheel of fortune, a genuine alligator and boa-constrictor, with the background music of 'Pop Goes the Weasel'. Just in case anyone got too carried away, there were also Temperance meetings (including the Total Abstinence Society's soiree), open-air services, and meetings of the Linktown Mutual Improvement Society. The newly formed Linktown Instrumental Band, made up of pottery workers, made their debut at the Market in 1855 in their splendid new uniforms which were "a close approximation to that worn by the Hussars".

The early 1900s still brought merchandise direct from maker to buyer, as *Davidson's Guide to Kirkcaldy* pointed out in 1908. "The merchant met his customer at the market. Thus, as soon as one market was past, the tradesmen commenced making the articles he dealt in for the next he was to attend— boots and shoes (needless to say, more of the country road than the drawing room class), tattie creels, clothes and message baskets, from unpeeled, peeled or split willow mostly, some of them made on the spot by deft hands while you wait; tin pitchers, pans and dishes of every description; earthenware, brown and white (brown teapots being much in evidence.) The 'wee cooper o' Fife' too was there, with his tubs, pails and water stoups, with his white, green and black pots of paint to finish his job if you so desired."

The roundabout and other early rides were manually operated or horse-drawn, and an early photograph taken around 1900 shows Smith's Pony Circus, a roundabout operated by a patient pony walking round in a circle.

Credit for the first Swingboat in 1866 is said to go to Chris Macintosh, a travelling showman who set up a large wooden boat in a frame which was pulled from side to side by ropes, on a site near Buchanan Street. Some small rides for children continued to be operated by hand for many years (with a few manually turned by a handle like a domestic mangle surviving into the Fifties.) In the nineteenth and early twentieth centuries, horses still provided the main source of power. They were then superseded by the mighty traction engines which not only pulled the showmen's wagons and equipment but also generated enough steam to operate the rides and the fairground organs which provided the music of the day.

"The mechanical things were introduced about my time, after I started work about 14," recalled the late John Crichton, who was born in 1901. "Everything was drawn by horses—the showmen's caravans, all their gear, even the circuses. They grazed their horses in a field where the bus office is. They started bringing in amusements like merry-go-rounds, small ones for youngsters which were driven by turning a handle, and then all the other things were introduced gradually. The steam engine was stuck right in the middle of the merry-go-round and that made it work. They didn't have electric light then; there were paraffin lamps which were incandescent and which hung up underneath the stalls and flickered and spluttered with a naked flame. They had burners like a candle flame—yet I don't remember any accidents.

"There was a mechanical organ which played music through punched cards on rolls; that was steam driven, later on when traction engines did away with the horses. I remember once on a Saturday morning they had an

Carousels and other attractions set up in 1906 on the Sands Road. The uneven ground before the Prom was made up can be seen on the right of the picture, with a chip cart on the left.
(Fife Council Libraries)

10

organ tuner there testing the pipes, tuning it up; it was a marvellous instrument.

"There were taps to the nearest water point all down one side of the road, and men went about all day long wheeling water tubs, barrels on wheels, from the taps to the engines. They weren't very big engines so they needed feeding all the time, they needed coal too—there was lots of black smoke and when it turned wet, you were over the ankles in mud."

The *Fife Free Press* agreed about the mud; its report in 1913 described the conditions on the dusty Sands Road after heavy rain. "Though the weather cleared up in the afternoon, the roads did not. Go where you liked, it was all the same. Still a good many were there trailing through the mud some inches deep. Men went plodding on, their trousers turned far up, but still the mud splashed higher. As for the women, it was not sufficient to hold the dress up with one hand, it required two. On meeting an acquaintance that night, there was no need to ask if he had been at the market, his feet told the tale."

The scene of the earliest markets can only be imagined, but the period which spanned the end of the nineteenth and start of the twentieth centuries was undoubtedly the peak of fairground tradition in the grand style. Carousels, Swingboats, Gondolas and Scenic Railways were presented with all the lavishness and grandeur of the Victorian and Edwardian ages. The ornate hand-carved rides were painted in flamboyant golds, reds and purples, and the majestic steam organs played Scottish tunes, rousing marches, and popular songs of the day such as *Dolly Gray* and *Two Lovely Black Eyes*. No expense was spared to provide magnificent rides and entertainments which were eagerly anticipated before the Market and talked about long after it had

A touch of old Venice was brought to the Links Market in 1896 with another of Wilmot's popular rides, the Gondolas. The family name can be seen painted on the lamps.
(Fife Council Museums: Kirkcaldy Museum and Art Gallery)

11

John Evans advertised the introduction of his Scenic Railway in the *Fife Free Press* of 1913.

left town. The same showmen's families came to the same pitches at the Links Market every year, including well known names such as Wilmot, Codona, Taylor, White, Evans and Pinder, with many of these families still coming to Kirkcaldy today.

The introduction of electricity meant that even more spectacular rides appeared on the scene. The splendour of that golden age was perhaps summed up by the Scenic Railway which John Evans brought to Kirkcaldy for the first time in 1913. It was such a striking innovation that it was recalled fondly by one local man some sixty years after he saw it as a boy. "The Evans family had a huge Scenic Railway which was built up with beautiful scenery done up with a waterfall which pumped real water. It was lovely, and it had a mechanical organ which provided the music." Evans was so proud of his new attraction that he took out an advert on the front page of the *Fifeshire Advertiser* in the week before the Market. "First Visit to Kirkcaldy!" it ran. "Grand new Scenic Railway costing £9,500 will be erected at the wide space, west end of the Sands Road on Thursday evening, and will be open to the people of Fife on Friday and Saturday. This novel railway is the largest and best of its kind owned by any amusement caterer in Great Britain. No steam engines employed. Each car driven by electricity. Beautiful scenery, including waterfalls and forests. Everyone will enjoy a ride on this gorgeous railway." Even allowing for possible poetic licence, a fairground ride costing £9,500 (including £2000 for the organ alone) in the year before the First War, just had to be seen to be believed.

**John Evans'
spectacular Scenic
Railway**
(National Fairground
Archive)

Stalls set up around 1900 selling Streimer's French nougat, ginger beer and other goodies. One of Wilmot's living wagons stands on the right.
(Fife Council Museums: Kirkcaldy Museum and Art Gallery)

And seen it most certainly was. An estimated crowd of 3000 people gathered at the west end of the Sands Road on the Thursday evening to watch members of the Town Council cut the red, white and blue ribbons across the entry to open the ride officially. "The Councillors took their seats in the richly upholstered cars and the signal was given that all was ready," reported that week's *Fifeshire Advertiser*. "The control box (cut from a section of a monster tree in Australian style) was occupied by Judge Peebles, who firmly switched on the electric power and the train of cars moved smoothly away, passing up hill and down dale through the fairy landscapes and under the rushing cascade. The speed was gradually increased until the indicator pointed to 40 miles an hour. After three hearty cheers, the party adjourned to Mr Evans' beautiful mahogany travelling van, where they were hospitably entertained by Mr and Mrs Evans." After several toasts were proposed, free rides were given to hundreds of children, to their "unmeasured delight". The railway was, unsurprisingly, the smash hit of that year's Market, with "enormous numbers of people of all ages and conditions" sampling the ride for themselves. "It may be mentioned," added the newspaper, "that on Monday evening, the Scenic Railway will be in full operation and the entire proceeds will be generously handed over to the funds of Kirkcaldy Hospital".

John Evans' generosity to the people of the town was only one example of the regular donations made by the showpeople. In 1908, for instance, John Wilmot gave £8 (a considerable sum in these days) to the Poor's Fund, £2 to the Cottage Hospital and £1 to the Female Mission, a charity also supported by Walter Wilmot, Mrs Pinder from the Circus, and McIndoe's cinematograph show. In 1911 John Wilmot was reported as "handing over, as usual, £2 to Kirkcaldy Hospital and £3 to the poor of the Burgh". When the local Cottage Hospital still relied on donations from the public, the Showmen's Guild collected money each year from the Market tenants and presented it to the Hospital Pageant committee.

In those days, the Market started up on the Thursday night, with no official opening ceremony (Scenic Railways aside) as there is today. One of the best-loved traditions, which was taken up with overwhelming enthusiasm, was that the first ride was given free of charge to children. As early as 1898, a reporter from the *Fife Free Press* recorded his eyewitness account of the happy chaos of the free ride on John Wilmot's roundabout. "Girls first—and it was with difficulty the boys were kept back. When every girl was settled it started, every place filled, and some horses seating two. All too soon the ride came to an end and it was the boys' chance. Coming over on the road was a dark sea of boys, jostling and straining forward and, like a dam that had broken its banks, flowed up over everything. Nothing could be seen but boys, two and three deep on the horses, while the Gondolas were one heaped mass, and even then the attendants had to fling themselves forward and bar the flood which still flowed on. As they whirled around the hurrahing and waving of caps commenced and continued to the end. After this round was finished, up went the card with 'One Penny' on it."

The huge traction engines which brought the showmen into town were majestic examples of engineering (and those which survive today still command an enthusiastic following when they appear at fairs and rallies). Occasionally, however, they caused traffic accidents which must have been as spectacular as the engines themselves. In 1913, two separate incidents took place when steam engines pulling their train of wagons went out of control on the Kirkcaldy streets. The first happened on the Path—always a steep hill and a notorious hazard for traffic even after it had been straightened and improved on several occasions, including 1902 when it became a tram

The junction of Heggie's Wynd and the newly made Esplanade was packed with crowds at the 1926 Market, showing a sea of flat caps. Lovett's hobby horses can be seen on the right hand side.
(Fife Council Libraries)

route. John Evans' engine with four heavily-laden wagons—perhaps carrying his new railway—had just passed Nairn's offices when the load became too much for the engine to hold. The entire cavalcade slid down the steep Path, turned completely round and crashed into a wall demolishing a large part of it and bringing the traffic to a halt.

The next day on the other side of town, one of John Wilmot's traction engines came to grief at the junction of Whytehouse Avenue and the High Street. The driver tried to avoid colliding with a car and pulled his engine to the side of the road. His wagons however toppled over and smashed the large plate glass window of Graham's China Warehouse on the corner of High Street, doing £10 worth of damage to the window display. One of the wagons was itself practically demolished, but fortunately the driver escaped injury and there were no pedestrians on the pavement at the time.

The Market closed down for the duration of both World Wars. The *Fife Free Press* of 1915 reported that "the bairns, young maidens and their sweethearts, and the old folks are this year to be deprived of the Links Market, the Magistrates having decided that owing to the war it would not be advisable to hold the fair, so brilliantly lit up in the evening, on the sea front. Several of the amusement caterers asked permission to put their attractions at the open space at Caledonian Mills, but this request has been refused". Once hostilities had ceased, local people welcomed the return of the colour, noise and spectacle with delight; although no-one could forget the past few years. Indeed, the local paper provided a sombre reminder with a description of the shooting gallery which now "gave outlet for the prowess of the demobilised soldier who has become a marksman since the last Fair, and who transferred his rifle practice from shooting Huns to breaking bottles, valuable as they now are".

Advertisement for Wilmot's Enterprises in the *Fife Free Press* of 1913

The official opening ceremony in 1969 with Provost Nicholson and his wife, members of the Showmen's Guild, and Town Council officials.
(Fife Council Museums: Kirkcaldy Museum and Art Gallery)

The once-traditional scramble for a free ride after the official opening in 1969.
(Fife Council Museums: Kirkcaldy Museum and Art Gallery)

During the Second War, the question of whether or not the Market should stay open was the subject of a heated debate in the Town Council Chamber in April 1940. The Provost asked for a statement on the safety aspect from Chief Constable Baldie, who stressed the danger of closing the road for the best part of a week, which could hamper the movement of ARP or military personnel should there be an air-raid. Buses would have to be rerouted to unaccustomed routes in the blackout, leading to increased likelihood of accidents. Most of all, he pointed out the danger of the lights from the lines of caravans strung along the foreshore, making the town an easy target for enemy aircraft. His viewpoint was supported by Provost Wilson, but some of the Councillors disagreed and made a strong case for keeping the Market open to keep up the morale of the people who, they felt, needed something to lift their spirits. After a long discussion, it was decided by 18 votes to 10 to hold the Market as usual, but with the reservation that it would be closed each evening half an hour before the blackout came into force. It was to be the only Market held for five years.

John Evans's front page advert in the *Fife Free Press* of 1920

And of course the showmen, like the Market visitors and those in every walk of life, were in active service in both wars. The Showmen's Guild also tirelessly raised funds to help the war effort. During the First War, fifteen ambulances were bought for the Red Cross by the Guild and its members, at a time when fairs were closed for the duration and many of the showmen's traction engines had been requisitioned by the War Office. In 1940, an appeal was published in *The World's Fair* (the showmen's weekly newspaper) to raise funds to buy a Spitfire or Hurricane fighter plane for the Royal Air Force. The original idea gathered momentum and within a year the target figure of £5000 was raised to buy a Spitfire which was named *The Fun of the Fair*. The plane was damaged in active service but after the war it was used in technical training until it was scrapped in 1953.

When the lights came on again on the Esplanade in 1946, the rides and sideshows came out of mothballs to a rapturous reception, even though there were few new attractions until the following year. The reappearance of bright lights, noise and colour from the Tiel Burn along the length of the Prom was warmly welcomed, as the circuses, dive-bombers, rocket cars, coconut shies and side-stalls took up their usual stances.

Although the Baillies and Town Councillors used to take a stroll round the Market on the Friday evening around the turn of the century, there was no official start to the Market apart from the free rides. In 1950 a new tradition was set up, when the Provost, Councillors and representatives of the Showmen's Guild carried out an opening ceremony on the Wednesday afternoon, and this has been kept up ever since. The first official ceremony was carried out by Provost James Young, who toured the site and then at 3 p.m. declared the Market open and made the long-awaited announcement,

"Free rides for all!" Local youngsters used to hold the popular if cynical belief that the free rides were to see if everything was in good working order. "The market was free for the first hour. This was to test to see if we would be killed—but we didn't care, we were off like dafties!" Although the scramble for the first free ride has now been discontinued, no doubt on safety grounds, the official party make a practice of walking through the fairground after the opening ceremony, distributing tickets for free rides amongst the spectators.

Another long-held tradition is the Market lunch, held in a local hotel on the Wednesday, with Fife Council and the Showmen's Guild taking it in turns to host the event. Guests include those working behind the scenes, representatives from the local community, and people who have played their part over the years in making the event run smoothly. After a short session of speeches, the official party drive down to the Prom accompanied by a police escort, to carry out the opening ceremony.

Building programmes or road improvements have made little difference to the Market, which has carried on serenely, letting the work proceed round about it. In 1923, for instance, when the old Sands Road was being levelled out and turned into the Prom in what would now be called a jobs creation scheme, the rides were set up there all the same. The *Fife Free Press* of the day commented sternly: "It is worthy of note that despite the great transformation that has been effected on the sea front of the town, work in connection with which is not yet completed, the fair is being held as usual there. In passing, the hope can only be expressed that their presence, with the multitude of people the shows attract, will not result in any damage to work that is progressing, or interference with the contractor's plant."

And in 1956, when a major demolition exercise was carried out on the Prom—including knocking down Viewforth Tower, an eighteenth century mansion designed by Kirkcaldy-born Robert Adam—to build the eight-storey

When the high flats were under construction in 1956, the Market continued regardless.
(Fife Council Libraries)

flats, it was business as usual despite the JCBs and cement mixers nearby. Or almost as usual, as the *Fife Free Press* pointed out: "A dozen showmen will not be able to sit back once their stalls have been erected. Their stances are directly before the entrance to the partly-completed eight-storey flats, and they will have to erect their stalls at 6 pm every day and dismantle them before midnight till the market closes on Monday."

From time to time there have been proposals to site the Market away from the Prom. At the 1957 opening ceremony, Provost David Wright said: "Some people are tinkering with the idea of taking it to some field. I am one who has had some experience of a fair in a field, and I can tell you that in wet weather it be becomes a veritable quagmire. In the Links, the market is on solid ground and I hope it will always remain in this area."

Three years later however, Kirkcaldy Town Council considered the request by Councillor John Kay to move the event half a mile inland to Beveridge Park. Councillor Kay said at the time: "There is a tarmac roadway that runs in a large semi-circle from one side of the park to the other, almost linking Balwearie Road and Boglily Road. It is well clear of the flower gardens, and if that thoroughfare were widened up to 50 feet, the actual market attractions could stand on the solid surface which could also be traversed by the public. The various trailers and living caravans could be parked on the grass verge.

"There are some who may hold up their hands in horror," he added with considerable understatement, "both at the break with tradition and the thought of havoc being created in the park, but they need not worry. The effects, if any, of the Market in April would be completely eradicated by May, when the park is becoming popular again for the summer season. It is

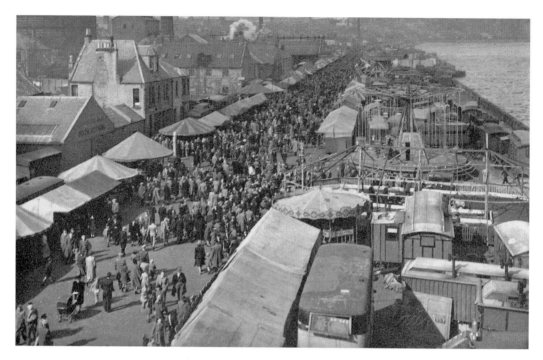

my contention that rents revenue from the resited Market should go to the Parks Department, and I was assured that this would not only pay for tidying up the park but would finance an improvement programme for the vacated Esplanade.

"The whole area is an eyesore for 51 weeks of the year because the one-week Market precludes any beautification plans. A transfer of the showmen to the park should solve all that, and it would also eliminate the need to close a main roadway for ten days, aggravating traffic congestion that is bad enough at the best of times."

His plan however was not approved, and although he put forward an alternative suggestion that the site should be altered to extend the full length of the Esplanade but on the seaward side only, this was not taken up either.

Another unsuccessful attempt to re-site the event—this time in the Gallatown Stadium at Randolph Road—was made in 1971. Building development, increase in traffic, and bigger fairground trailers and caravans were all given as reasons for a move, together with the inconvenience of closing the Prom to traffic for ten days. In 1993, as the Esplanade underwent another phase of upgrading, continuing on the traditional site was again viewed with needless pessimism.

The notorious Market weather has sometimes caused very real disruption to the showmen's equipment. In 1960, for instance, fierce gales ripped the entire canvas top of Pinder's International Circus to shreds—but in true show tradition, a new big top was hastily put up in its

place so that the circus could open in time. The same storm lifted up a 30 ft long coconut shy belonging to William Cullis and hurled it against the door of one of the family's living wagons.

In 1994, a plaque commemorating the existence of a market on the Links of Abbotshall since 1304 was placed near Buchanan Court in a joint venture by Kirkcaldy Civic Society and the Scottish Section of the Showmen's Guild. It was officially unveiled by the late Joe Richard White, then 90 years old, whose family have been coming to the Market for generations.

Opening hours have altered on several occasions over the years. In 1964, for example, it started up at 10 a.m. on the Saturday morning instead of noon, to suit the changing work patterns of most people in the town who were by then on a five day week. Another change took place ten years later, when the Guild asked that the Market should open on a Sunday afternoon, to help offset an increase of 40 per cent ground rental. The Town Council agreed to the Guild's request, and the Market operated on a Sunday for the first time in 1974, with the decision taken by both the Council and the Guild that there would be no music.

Local shops and businesses in Kirkcaldy used to have a good increase in trade from the showmen, probably more so than in the present time— although corner shops in Links Street still cope well with urgent requests for 14 lbs of sugar to re-stock a candy floss machine. Coachbuilders such as Marshall and Chudy in Kirkcaldy and Carr's of Buckhaven built or repaired showmen's caravans. Repairs to the circus poles and stalls were carried out by local joiners such as Geordie Muir whose workshop was in Ramsay Road and who also supplied sawdust for the floors of some of the stalls. In earlier days, clay pipe 'seconds' from Lowrie's factory on the Sands Road were used as targets in shooting galleries or to throw wooden balls at, and dishes and mugs from Methven's Pottery in Links Street were sold from traders' stalls. The donkey rides for youngsters, on ground near the Tiel Burn, were operated by a local farmer from the Boreland.

All the shops in the area were patronised by the showmen. "My Dad's cousin had a fruit and vegetable shop in the Fifties opposite the Rialto in the High Street—she used to get in a basket of Scotch tomatoes for the Market," remembered one local man. "They used to be 7/6 a lb., which was very dear at the time, but she always got them sold to the Market people, they were the only ones who could afford them!" The showmen took their dry cleaning to Halley's Dyeworks and bought their families new shoes at Mathieson's shoe shop.

Alexander's buses were kept busy during the Market period. "When we finished our shifts at the garage at Buckhaven," recalled one former conductress, "they turned us about back into Kirkcaldy to pick up stragglers to bring them home in the early hours of the morning. This was in the

Fifties when not so many people would have cars, and every bus that was available was sent into Kirkcaldy where we used to wait at the west end of the High Street."

Local bakers and confectioners in the 1900s, such as J & A Kidd in Rosslyn Street, William McCathie at 175 High Street (near where Littlewoods store stands now) and Robbie Salmond in the High Street supplied the gingerbread, sweets wrapped in silver and gold paper, and sugar hearts in all sizes, which were all part of Market tradition. Or as local poet A.B. Paton put it in his poem 'I'm a Links Laddie!' in 1910:

At the Market I've bocht parlies, or sometimes some ging'bread men
There were no sae mony swey-boats or steam habbie-horses then;
An we laughed when Robbie Salmond got some muckle country loon
An' filled his hat wi' ging'bread an' then knocked it oot th' croon.

Even in the 1950s, Jock Mackie whose baker's shop was in Carlyle Road, provided gingerbread and sweets for the hungry crowds. One local man

Friday afternoons were traditionally the time when mothers wheeled their babies in high prams round the Market, as shown in this 1910 postcard, in what was popularly known as the Baby Show or Baby Parade. Schools also closed early on Fridays to let older children enjoy the fun. A chip cart and the Helter-skelter are also pictured.
(Fife Council Libraries)

said: "I remember when Jock, who had a tuck shop at the old High School, made sweeties at a stall near Volunteers' Green. He boiled sugar in different colours, and when it was ready he took balls of different colours of the hot sugar and threw them on to a hook where they slowly dripped off. He would catch the mixture as it fell and threw it back on to the hook again and gradually mixed it all up enough to make hard boilings. Not very good for our teeth, but we loved them."

Several types of entertainment which carried on until the 1950s and 60s have now disappeared in a mixture of changing tastes, political correctness and sometimes health and safety issues. Pinder's two circuses, with lions, clowns, acrobats and an elephant, are no longer in their traditional stance in the basin at the west end of the Esplanade. The chance to have your photograph taken with a monkey dressed up in a little suit is not now on offer. 'Freak' shows too have disappeared, with their exhibits which included the Half Woman and Half Beast, The Lady with Three Legs, The Living Skeleton, The Lobster Claw Man, and as one local poet put it at the time: "Some queer like specimens there we saw, o' men ower big an' men ower

sma'." The cinematographs or bioscopes, which gave displays of moving pictures before the days of cinema or television, were phased out as more modern technology came into people's homes. Even the boxing booths, which still drew crowds in the Sixties, are just memories—but vivid ones at that, as many people still remember cheering on local champions and watching the braver (or more foolhardy) men in the crowd taking up the challenges of stepping into the ring.

Friday afternoons are no longer the favourite time for mothers to dress their children in their best and wheel them round the Market in high prams in what was known as the Baby Show—as well as for older children who got the afternoon off school. Traders' stalls, which once stretched in double lines over large areas of the Prom and up the narrow wynds off Links Street, have all gone. Silver-tongued salesmen who offered bargains in china, household linen, and kitchen gadgets have disappeared into the sunset. The traditional market sweets which were presented to wives and girlfriends as tokens of affection, have been replaced by candy floss, toffee apples, hot dogs, pasta and smart coffee bars.

The years pass: and the Market moves on with the changing times.

Chapter 2
Behind the Scenes

Most visitors to the Links Market probably give little thought to the planning, organisation and sheer hard work which goes on beforehand—but a large annual event like this doesn't 'just happen.' Kirkcaldy has always prided itself on the high level of co-operation and friendship which exists between the local authority and the showmen at the Links Market—something which is still very much in evidence today.

From the days of Kirkcaldy Town Council, through Kirkcaldy District Council and now Fife Council, the setting up and running of the Market in conjunction with the Showmen's Guild has always run smoothly and harmoniously.

This 1950s view shows the Market layout as well as many old buildings, now demolished, on Links Street and the Prom.
(Fife Council Libraries)

Allocating each showman his correct space on the Prom, collecting the site rents, liaising with the Police and Fire services, providing water hydrants, postal service and first aid post, rerouting traffic and putting up direction signs are just some of the background work which must be carried out efficiently each year. White marks are painted on the kerb all the way along the road to mark out each person's ground, with every ride or sideshow built precisely between the marks.

The Market itself is traditionally fixed for the Wednesday before the third Friday in April; sometimes this coincides with Easter weekend or the local school holidays, depending on the timing of Easter itself. The actual Market period now lasts for ten days, with the Prom being closed to other traffic before each year's event from midnight on the Saturday until midnight the following Tuesday.

Until fairly recently it was the job of the Market Superintendent (often a retired police officer) to oversee all the arrangements, and both the *Fife Free Press* and *The World's Fair* have never been slow to praise his efforts.

One of the showmen commented in 1910: "We take our ground from the town at a living rental under the able supervision of Mr Gatherum, the chief constable, efficiently supported by Inspector Rhynd who allots our positions. We all take our hats off to him in admiration of his tact, firmness and discernment in dealing with over a mile of showmen." And *The World's Fair* reported in 1936: "One can but imagine the colossal task that confronts

Building up the Market at the Basin in 1962 including the two Big Tops of Pinder's circuses.
(Edwin Pinder)

This fine painting of the Links Market by James Patrick is dated 1884 and is in the collection of Kirkcaldy Museums and Art Gallery. The scene is the Sands Road with Swingboats, side stalls and chip carts. The imposing Viewforth Towers on the left was designed by world famous Kirkcaldy-born architect Robert Adam. It was demolished in 1956 and replaced with eight-storey flats.

(Fife Council Museums: Kirkcaldy Museum and Art Gallery)

the Market Superintendent. That all tenants line up in their allotted space with their respective outfits and everything is apple-pie order on opening day, is undoubtedly a tribute to ex-Det. Sgt. Nelson. He has always taken a personal interest in individual requirements, and bestows much time and patience on the many problems that arise. With many showmen now owning big machines, there is the incessant call for more space, and it is no easy matter securing extra elbow room unless it be to the disadvantage of the small man. The Town Officials lay down certain rules and regulations in connection with the Market, but Mr. Nelson never takes up the role of the dictator. Long association with Scottish showpeople has formed many friendships and the knowledge of their difficulties often smooths out matters with the Town's officials."

Ten years later, Alex Nelson was still carrying out the job, and *The World's Fair* described him as "still hale and hearty and as keenly interested as ever in the big event. The setting out of stances and endeavouring to please everyone is a herculean task, but the ex-detective sergeant always manages to get things shipshape, despite the fact that he is well over 70. For the last year or two he has been thinking about laying aside his measuring tape and paint pot, and stresses the fact that next year will possibly be the final occasion on which he will act as Market officer." He eventually retired in 1950, when the Showmen's Guild made a presentation to him in recognition of 20 years' service.

Part of the Market site map showing the marked stances near the Basin

Another police officer who took up the post of Market Superintendent on his retirement was ex-Depute Chief Constable William Hunter. He held

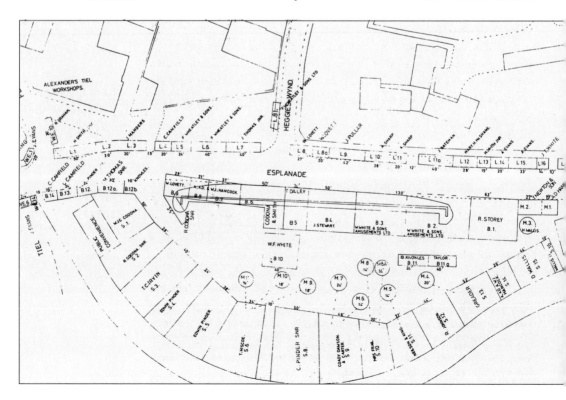

the post for fifteen years until his death in 1965. His obituary in the *Fife Free Press* said: "He was well known personally to hundreds of showmen and their families throughout the country. He spared no effort to bring the latest and best attractions to Kirkcaldy, and at the time of his death he was in the midst of final preparations for this year's Market, the 661st. His duties as Market Superintendent called for organising ability of a high order, as well as a keen appreciation of the modern trends in the field of entertainment, and the wide experience he gained in the course of his police career stood him in good stead."

At that year's Market—surely a poignant occasion only a fortnight after his death—several tributes were paid to him. "Due to Mr Hunter's ability and organisation, the letting and setting of the hundreds of sites was accomplished to the satisfaction of all concerned," said George William Smith of the Showmen's Guild. "He was a dedicated person as far as the Links Market was concerned, always striving to keep it Europe's greatest fair, with the greatest variety of showground equipment to entertain the public.

"I personally admired his setting out of the fair, which is a huge task for anyone, and I often wondered how he managed to accommodate all his tenants. It will be strange to many who will look along the Market not to see his tall commanding figure walking along the Links, as he was an integral part of this event."

He was succeeded at very short notice by John Lawson (who served in the First War and then in India, retiring with the rank of Major) who had retired four years previously from the Burgh Engineer's Department in Kirkcaldy Town House. In an interview in his first year of office, he said: "The work starts in the first week of December, when I book the equipment, plan the various sites on maps, and write to all the big Market families to give them their positions. After I have obtained applications for stances, it's my job to plot each piece of equipment on the site map. The applicants are then told that they will have a stance at L1 or GG5 or wherever, and they know exactly where to go. On the seaward and landward sides, the numbers reach 90, which means that there are well over 200 pieces of equipment when the Market is in full swing. After that, it's up to the public to make the event a success or a failure."

Fife Council's current man behind the Market's successful setting up is John Haggart, Fife Council Community Services Officer, who has been in post since 1995. "I co-ordinate all the various services, both internal and external including the Showmen's Guild. I suppose you could call me a focal point where all the difference services and organisation come together," he said.

"There's still very much a feeling of co-operation and friendship between Fife Council and the Showmen's Guild. We've developed a very good working relationship with the Showmen's Guild, police and fire services, with a good line of communication and co-operation among us all, which means that the whole thing is co-ordinated in a much more efficient way."

The working master-plan of the Links Market site is a fascinating

John Haggart (left) Fife Council's Community Services Officer was on site as the rides were built up on Sunday morning at the 2003 Market.
(Andrew Beveridge, Fife Council)

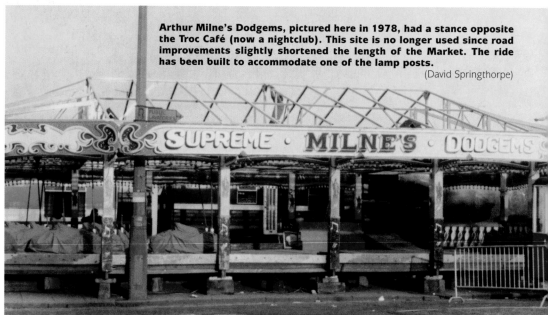

Arthur Milne's Dodgems, pictured here in 1978, had a stance opposite the Troc Café (now a nightclub). This site is no longer used since road improvements slightly shortened the length of the Market. The ride has been built to accommodate one of the lamp posts.
(David Springthorpe)

Showmen's living wagons were packed together at the west end of the Prom in 1986.
(Nancy Brodie)

Philip Paris, Chairman of the Scottish Section of the Showmen's Guild in 2003, pictured with two of his entertainments, a teacup roundabout for children and his amusement arcade on the right.
(Andrew Beveridge, Fife Council)

document: a long thin map which unrolls endlessly to document each ride and side-stall on the 950-metre site on the Prom. Each allocation of ground is meticulously marked with the area leased to each showman, with generations of the same family often occupying the same site year after year.

"Planning the event takes perhaps six months with varying degrees of intensity, starting with a couple of hours in the week initially up until the actual operation of the Market when I am on-site all the hours there are," said John Haggart. "We have our first operations meeting in December, but before that I do background work necessary for public order, public safety, leases for caravan sites, and seeing to specifications for new Health and Safety requirements."

A year after John Haggart took up the post, a policy change made the Showmen's Guild responsible for the lease of the whole site. "In practice, this means that the Guild pays Fife Council for the site and then they charge and collect individual ground rents from their members—which makes one part of my job very much easier.

"Fife Council operate it so that it isn't a profit-making event; it breaks even and if there is a surplus, it's used against any deficit in coming years. The public doesn't subsidise the operating costs, and the revenue from the event goes into the Common Good Fund."

Philip Paris, Chairman of the Scottish Section of the Showmen's Guild at the time of writing, agreed that the Council and the Guild continue to work well together. He has been involved behind the scenes since 1997 and more recently in a key capacity. "For the last five years I have been the Main Steward, the main person responsible from the Showmen's Guild," Philip Paris said. "This means I can't leave the site without leaving a deputy in charge, and I liaise with Fife Council, the police and fire service, Health and Safety, and anyone else necessary. People seem to think we just roll up at places at a given time, but there's a lot of organisation behind it all and the Links Market meetings go on for months before the event.

Logo of the Showmen's Guild of Great Britain which was founded in 1889

"The recent changes mean that we now have the lease for the Prom at that particular time of year, and rental is charged at so much per foot, with different charges on the different types of equipment. We take all the applications from the operators of the various equipment, and we are responsible for collecting all the safety certificates and insurance certificates. If police overtime is involved, the cost of that is passed on to us, as is the cost of cleaning up the site afterwards.

"The Showmen's Guild is very strictly run, with the Scottish section one of ten sections within the Guild, and the Chairman of our section is elected every year at our annual general meeting in November. Our Rule Book has been part of the Guild since its inception in 1889—it's like a

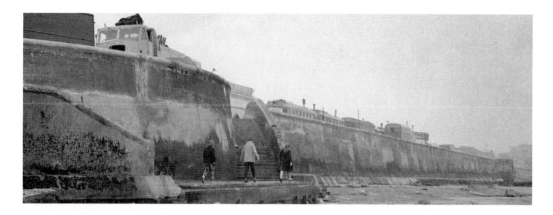

Living wagons parked up against the sea wall can be seen in this view from the foreshore
(Fife Council Libraries)

code of practice which covers members' conduct, safety standards which are paramount in our business with the equipment tested annually by an independent engineer, public liability insurance, and so on. A showman who owns a ride and who employs staff, for instance, is responsible for the conduct of his staff.

"We have a very well organised procedure if there is a complaint by one member against another; the case is heard and the person can be fined and ordered to obey the rules in future. If they are not satisfied with the decision, it goes to the appeals committee as a complete re-hearing, and after that there is a final right of appeal where a QC is in attendance. Our members are encouraged to go through the procedure of the Showmen's Guild before taking it to a civil court of law, and most cases can be worked out that way.

"Another basic part is our rule of Established Rights, which essentially means that a show family has the right to a particular spot in the Market, carried forward from generation to generation. Although I rent the stance I have here from Fife Council, it is recognised within the Guild as my stance as long as I comply with the Guild rules, so another showman couldn't just come along and move on to it. We can however make arrangements to transfer sites from one tenant to another, so long as both are in agreement.

"The Showmen's Guild members run businesses just like any others, except that we're not always in the same place like 'flatties,' as we call people who are outwith the fairground business. This business has changed a lot in recent years, with lots of pressures, rules and regulations—it's becoming harder to earn a living out of it.

"About four years ago we had a committee of MPs looking into the fairgrounds. They took a lot of evidence and basically what they said was that it would be a very foolish Council who said that the fairground business was coming to the end or had no future. As far as they could see in the evidence, it was a flourishing business—they really gave the Guild great recognition. Since I've been Chairman of the Scottish section, we've been trying to get some sort of representation in the Scottish Parliament. We have an all-party group of MPs in Westminster, but nothing like that in the Scottish Parliament so far. As most of the legislation that would affect us as showmen in Scotland would come from there, I have had some meetings already and

A showman's wagon owned by Jimmy Graham in 1978.
(David Springthorpe)

Teamwork is the basis of successful preparation and building up before each Market.
(Andrew Beveridge, Fife Council)

Building up some of the rides at the 2003 Market.
(Andrew Beveridge, Fife Council)

John Codona's boldly decorated lorry is pictured at the 1978 Market.
(David Springthorpe)

This view of the rides and wagons in the Basin was taken from the high flats in 1978. The mouth of the Tiel Burn and the bus garage can also be seen.
(David Springthorpe)

A wooden Molycroft wagon pictured around 1910 showing Lizzie Dick with her daughters Teenie and Cissie sitting on the steps. The cylinder on the right was part of the family's shooting stall.
(William Dalgleish)

hope to have more. Recently we hosted a reception in Edinburgh and asked all the MSPs to come along, although only a small number actually attended. We gave out an information pack which outlined some of the problems showmen come up against, such as public entertainment licencing for fairgrounds, and the need for a simplified system for getting planning permission for our yards or depots for the winter months."

The length of the Market has remained substantially the same for very many years. "The only real changes to the layout were when the multi-storey car park on the Prom was built and then when the road alignment was changed to continue Nicol Street down to the Prom," said John Haggart. "These roadworks meant that we lost the spaces for six machines and about 35 small stalls, but apart from that the length has remained the same, 950 metres. Before then it would have been closer to a mile from the Troc Café to the Basin. We have two natural boundaries, from the diversionary route down Nicol Street along to the Bus Company property near the Tiel Burn. People keep thinking that the Market is shorter than it used to be, but apart from these minimal changes, it remains basically the same size."

A major change came in 1994 when the showmen's living wagons—until then parked on the Prom itself—were moved off the Market site under new Health and Safety regulations. Understandably, the move was initially not at all welcomed by the showmen who were accustomed to have their living quarters beside their equipment for both convenience and security.

"I can understand why this was seen as an unpopular move," said John Haggart. "Showmen and their families now have to walk a fair distance to get to and from their equipment from their living wagon, and this is obviously not so convenient especially when there are elderly members in the family. The Market is very much a family affair and often there are three or four pieces of equipment looked after by different people. A lot of local people and visitors liked the caravans there too—they added to the whole attraction and gave a glimpse of the showmen's way of life.

"It was entirely a Health and Safety directive, and with people living in the wagons it means there's gas and electricity, diesel from the generator lorries, wooden structures as well as metal ones, all the side stalls with a lot of canvas, and huge amounts of gloss paint—all typical fire hazards. The fire service, as well as providing the cover to put out any potential fire, go down each year with a fire prevention team and give out leaflets, information and advice on safety measures."

Philip Paris admitted that the decision to take the wagons off the site had not been a popular one with Guild members. "We did feel a bit aggrieved but we have to accept the safety aspects of it, and I don't think there's going to be any possibility of it changing back again," he said. "At most fairgrounds, people's wagons would be at the back of their equipment, and if older members of the family or young children were there, they could run their business and look after the family at the same time. It probably has kept some of our older people from coming to the Market now—they are more likely to stay settled in Glasgow in the winter quarters."

"The showmen start arriving on the Saturday afternoon when they bring their loads and leave them in the Basin car park," said John Haggart. "If all the English people arrive at the same time as the Scottish showmen, there can be a lot of congestion especially if it coincides with Raith Rovers playing at home, or Kirkcaldy Rugby Club at Beveridge Park. The police and I are down there on the Saturday to monitor the situation; there's a snack bar there and we can't allow their business to be affected by too many lorries parking there. If space is tight, sometimes the showmen have to wait in lay-bys outside the town.

Manning a ride is very much a family affair, with a young member of the Codona family helping out in the pay booth in 1988.
(Fife Council Museums: Kirkcaldy Museum and Art Gallery)

"The Prom closes at midnight on Saturday, and some of the showmen might go in then and leave their lorries on the grass or the car parks so that they can start building at 7 a.m. the next morning. I'm down there until about 2 a.m. to make sure there is no early building up because the local residents want a full night's sleep. There are occasional exceptions: the owner of one large Roller Coaster needs to hire a crane which is very expensive, so he has to have the groundwork prepared beforehand. He's allowed to put up the base stand, which has to be done with theodolites, on the Saturday night ready for the crane early the next morning."

The pull-on to the Prom on the Sunday morning is an eye-opener for anyone who is accustomed to seeing the Market only when it is up and running. The Prom's usual role as one of the main thoroughfares through Kirkcaldy changes overnight and becomes a fairground in the making, with a scene of constant activity and movement as the long lorries go back and forth to manoeuvre to get into their proper position. Many of the showmen, particularly those who are first-time tenants, have their copy of the site map to hand and a measuring tape to make sure they are building up exactly within their own allotted spaces. It's no exaggeration to say that if one showman overlaps his spot by one inch, the whole of the Prom set-up is thrown out of kilter in a domino effect. "There's a bit of chaos in the morning trying to get set up, but it's organised chaos and it all comes together at the end of the day," said one showman.

Raymond Codona's Motorcycle Speedway was built around a lamp post in 1978.

(David Springthorpe)

The exterior of the Outer Limits Funhouse being set up in 2003.　　(Andrew Beveridge, Fife Council)

Strong winds at the 1985 Market meant that the top 'tilt' or canvas had to be removed by the operators from John Codona's Dodgems for safety reasons.
(David Springthorpe)

One of Horne's Pleasure Fairs' rides being set up at the 2003 Market
(Andrew Beveridge, Fife Council)

It's an obvious advantage to be as early on the site as possible, to get the maximum advantage of the free space available. A few rides are still built up by hand, such as a children's Helter-skelter using a spirit level and blocks of wood for a stable flat base, but these are the exception these days. Building up the rides, while not so labour intensive as in days gone by, still requires a great deal of muscle, concentration and very hard work. The majority of the rides are made to fit within the lorries which transport them, so that once the lorry is in position, the ride itself can fold down into place. Some of the larger rides need cranes to get them into position; the towering height of Big Ben, the Drop Zone or the Bomber arrive horizontally and are painstakingly raised into their upright positions.

One local man recalled: "The showmen didn't get in until first thing on Sunday morning. If you were on the Orrock Quarry road the night before, you would see all the lorries up around Kilrie waiting for midnight—that was the traditional road for years and years. They used to come rattling in, they made a fair bit of noise and it was known as the gold rush. A lot of the shows were up by lunchtime on the Sunday."

In 1962 the local paper commented: "This year for the first time the public will be able to witness the mass migration of showmen and their families to the sites allotted them by the Market Superintendent. This 'Gold Rush' as the showmen call it, was formerly made during the early hours of the morning to avoid congestion on the roads. This year the 'rush' will take place at 9 o'clock on Sunday morning."

Nancy Brodie, whose house overlooks the Prom, probably knows the timetable as well as any showman. "When Mr Hunter ran it, no-one was allowed in until 8 a.m. on the Sunday morning. They would be all lined up, stopped outside the town or parked along near Seafield, and we would get up and stand in our dressing gowns at the window to watch them come in," she said.

"If the weather is fair, they begin to build up immediately because they want to get on with the job. Sunday is the day for building up—although a few manage to sneak on early before the road is closed the night before. Early on Sunday mornings when they pull on and start work, the Prom is lined with people with their cameras recording them building up. On Mondays the showmen do any painting that's needed and on Tuesdays they try out the lights and the music. On the Tuesday morning you can see all the lorries and vans coming along, with diesel for the generators, rolls for the hot dogs, and apples for the toffee apples.

"On the second Monday night some of the rides close down early, depending where they're going on to, as they want to get all packed up. That's the night when we don't get much sleep because they're pulling down. There used to be all the hammering and banging and machines coming down after midnight, but it's not so bad now. So many of the big machines now seem to fold down off the lorry, and they just pack away again when they pull down at the end of the Market.

"The Market people leave all their rubbish tidy in boxes, and it used to be that the dogs would get there before they were taken away and pull it all out again. I must say that in the past few years the Council have been down with their bin lorries before the dogs get the chance, and by teatime on Tuesday night you wouldn't even know there had been a Market there."

Now that the caravans are no longer on the Prom, the show people can make a more leisurely way to their temporary living sites and can often arrive before the road is closed. "Once we pull on to the site, building up is very much quicker than it used to be—the actual time it takes to put the rides together is minute in comparison to what it used to be," Philip Paris said. "The difference is that life is moving on at a faster pace, so we have to keep up with it. Building up the big rides and pulling down at the end of the fair is still men's work, and no women would build up Waltzers or Big Wheels— there's a lot of heavy work involved and sometimes showmen employ casual labour to help out."

Each year brings new refinements to help the efficiency of the smooth running of the event. The whole site, for instance, is now divided into lettered sectors for instant identification should emergency services be needed. In 2003, two-foot high platforms were put in place at regular intervals for the police to stand on for better visibility: a minor alteration perhaps, but one which proved an immediate success. "The police try to find a balance between subtle unobtrusive policing with a certain amount of high visibility for the public's reassurance," said John Haggart. "By raising the policemen's height by two feet, they can see each other clearly from sector to sector across the sea of heads. They can immediately see if there are any trouble spots, points where a crush is developing, or any other problems. Although this was entirely a police innovation, we had a lot of positive feedback on the site from the public who approved of the idea.

"We have a practice emergency evacuation on Thursday afternoon, when we close down all the music the full length of the site. A group of us, including the police, the Showmen's Guild committee, and myself walk through the ground sector by sector, and we could have the entire site evacuated if need be within twelve minutes.

"It's essential to have advance procedures which could be implemented if necessary. In 2003 for instance, the police estimate was something like 50,000 visitors a day on the Prom, with a much heavier attendance of family groups through the day thanks to the school holidays and the untypical sunny weather, with more teenagers and youths at night. The numbers don't vary all that much—there is a finite amount of money and a finite amount of people—but the timing can alter depending on the weather and the Easter weekend."

Early on Tuesday morning at the end of the stay, the whole process of building up is reversed into pulling down, when the rides are dismantled, packed up and folded away. As the lorries rumble out of town, the town returns to normal—until next year.

Chapter 3
Fairground attractions

"When push-bikes came into fashion, not everyone could afford to buy one, so cycling was quite a novelty," recalled John Crichton. "The showmen got old bicycles and fixed them on a circular track, quite close together—not too far apart or they would get fewer customers. You had to pedal yourself round and round the track. There were coconut shies and anything you could throw a small wooden ball at. There was a clay pipe factory down at the Prom, and their seconds were used for the sideshows where you threw balls at the pipes to win a prize."

Until quite recently, the side shows were considered by many people to be the backbone of the Market, and it's easy to understand why. Games of skill or chance, with prizes such as the old favourites of a goldfish or a coconut were there for the winning. Side stalls included darts and rifle shooting, hoopla, painted clown heads which moved from side to side to catch a ball, and hooking ducks with a fishing rod. One of the oldest, simplest to operate and therefore ever-popular, was rolling the pennies. "You rolled a penny

Dick's 'shooter' in the 1900s when customers aimed at bottles on the top shelf. The front of the stall displayed the Royal coat of arms. To the right was a target gallery for wooden balls aimed at clay pipes (seconds from a local factory) which were displayed as teeth in comic faces. Pictured (from left) are Kate Clark, Davie Clark, Willie Clark, Lizzie Dick and Celie Clark.
(William Dalgleish)

down a wooden slot and if it landed on a numbered square you got the same number of pennies back—but it had to be right on the square or you didn't get anything," said one local woman. "Some had a bar of chocolate on the squares and if it landed on one, you got the chocolate. When we got back my brother and I would make a board so we could roll our own pennies at home."

Locals remembered a variety of sideshows. "There was the one which had cardboard cut-outs of football players and you had to knock them down with bean bags. You could win a coconut for throwing balls into a pail, although most of them bounced out again. Then there were the duck races, with about 12 ducks in a row, and you placed a bet on which one would win the race. You might win a sixpence, and you went off to spend it again."

As early as 1853, according to the *Fifeshire Advertiser*, there were sideshows such as shooting galleries, travelling theatres, conjuring tricks and "exact likenesses done by machinery". They were followed by flea circuses, with the audience standing round a table to watch fearless fleas racing each other on chariots or bicycles; exotic sounding goldfish maypoles and revolving dolls; conjurers, fortune-tellers and 'quacks' who offered cures for every ailment; donkey rides, halls of distorting mirrors; barrel organists with or without monkeys—the stalls were never-ending.

Bioscopes or cinematograph shows, which were the fairground version of silent movies and later 'the talkies', were very popular at the start of the twentieth century and first appeared at the Links Market around 1904, with often as many as five or six shows by different operators. The *Fife Free Press* of 1909 was bowled over by the new attraction, and said: "The majority of the shows are of the cinematograph order, and they are got up in a style of magnificence quite new to this district. The outside stages of these shows are as much superior to the old-fashioned exhibition in artistic effect as the electric light with which they are illuminated, surpasses the penny dip. They are also equipped with excellent fairground organs. At the extreme east end there

Advert for the Great Australian Circus and Lion Show in the *Fife Free Press* of 1938

Advert for Biddall's Cinematograph in the *Fifeshire Advertiser* of 1908

D is for Dawson's the great picture show

A for Amusement which you get when you go

W for Waiting, there's none of that here

S for the good steady picture and clear

O for Ovation the pictures receive

N for None Better, you say when you leave.

A right Bang up to Date show

Dawson means Novelty, Talent and the best of value

Poster advertising Dawson's bioscope around 1910.
(Elizabeth Carter)

are stationed two fine entertainments—Biddall's cinematograph exhibition and McIndoe's famous Scottish show, the latter containing 40 miles of animated pictures, many from films by the best makers."

They showed commercial films including Cowboys and Indians, contemporary murder trials, patriotic features, slapstick and Scottish favourites such as Harry Lauder with his well known songs. In addition, a camera man would film local events and people leaving Kirkcaldy works and factories and show them on the screen during the Market. "My grandfather Billy Codona used to travel with the shows in the summer and do the cinematograph in the winter months," recalled show-woman Minnie Paris. "They would advertise 'Come to the fair and see yourself on film' to make their audience. The first time most people would have seen any type of moving pictures was on the fairgrounds."

The exterior of the bioscopes were elaborately decorated with a stage out front, on which two or three young ladies known as paraders—in frills, flounces and picture hats—did an exhibition dance to attract customers to see the show inside. "My mother, grandmother and aunt used to dance the cakewalk on the stage outside the bioscope to get the people in," said show-woman Harriet Hanley. "The films were silent with a man playing the piano, so they had to make an attraction outside." Bioscopes were said to be one of the mainstays of the showground until the time of the First War and the coming of cinema's golden age.

The early 1900s brought along waxwork shows, with likenesses of historical or contemporary figures—or as a contemporary local poet described them:

Chip carts were a perennial attraction at the Market. This _c._1910 photograph shows Kate Clark behind the counter with her father Geordie Clark behind her and four young members of their family. Bob Dick's traction engine, _Princess Louise_, can be seen to the left.
(William Dalgleish)

Arranged in groups to represent
Some famous men or great event
But little did the subjects vary—
The execution o' Queen Mary.
And Nap the great in exile deein',
An' Solomon his judgement gie'in.
'Twud be no show withoot the Queen
that's Neddy's mither; and a wheen
O' ither folk o' royal bluid
While saints and sinners 'mang them stood
Some o' oor maist heroic sojers
An' famous statesmen, maistly dodgers.

Felici Paris, great-grandfather of Philip Paris, with his chip cart in the 1920s
(Philip Paris)

'Fortune-tellers' who read palms or gazed into crystal balls were regular attenders. The *Fife Free Press* in 1910 reported: "Those who would peer into the future have ample opportunity to do so, there being fortune-tellers galore, both palmists and crystal gazers, including quite a host of 'royalties' ranging from 'the Queen of Epping Forest who is the only one patronised by the crowned heads of the world' to the one and only 'Queen of Scotland'." Or as a more down to earth local put it ninety years later: "Gypsy Ruby Smith was a fortune teller—we all knew her, she lived in Kirkcaldy, but we paid our 3*d*. just the same."

"My father Tommy Newton had the famous Laughing Clowns stall and took it to Kirkcaldy for years," said show-woman Lilian White. "There were ten clowns and their heads went back and forth with a box with numbers in front of them. It was five balls for sixpence, and they used to have to try to throw the balls on the right numbers so that they made the numbers up to five or thirty. If you got the ball in at the right moment, you could score and you got the pick of the stall. My Dad was very fussy and his stall was always lovely with good prizes like cut glass, crystal and teasets.

"We also had Bingo and fishing globes; and my brother Tommy Newton, who is one of the oldest showmen still working, still has his Bingo stall."

Fishing globes—where spectators tried to throw ping-pong balls into narrow-necked fish bowls to win a goldfish—were just one of the many sideshows which offered the chance to win this traditional prize. "The Showmen's Guild now has strict rules concerning giving away goldfish as prizes," said Philip Paris. "There has to be an alternative on offer so that winners don't have to take one as a prize. You're not allowed to hang them up in bags any more and instead the fish are swimming round in large bowls until they are won. We buy exactly the same bags as you would get if you bought a fish from a pet shop, and the bags have to have information printed on them on how to look after the fish. If people are going round the showground on rides, they're encouraged to leave the fish in the water, take a ticket and then collect the goldfish when they're ready to go home.

HOOK A WALE

ONE WIN

Card given out to goldfish winners to collect their prize at the end of their stay.

"Fairgrounds are licenced, and some Councils or areas make it a condition of the licence that there will be no goldfish given as prizes, the same way as they won't allow circuses with live animals."

Some of the sideshows would not now be considered to come under the category of entertainment. On 15 April 1914, the Edinburgh to Aberdeen express collided with the engine of the Carlisle goods train just outside Burntisland station, resulting in the tragic death of the driver and fireman from the express, and injuries to 12 of its passengers. According to a contemporary account: "Clearing the wreckage and raising the loco took some days and gave residents and thousands of visitors an opportunity of observing the dexterity and skill with which such tasks are completed." For those who had not gone to the scene, there was a tented exhibition at the Market within a few days of the Burntisland Train Disaster, with photographs of the crash and the rescue operation.

In 1930, the side-stalls included a display of a submarine safety device, which was fixed on to the conning tower. The *Fife Free Press* explained: "Should the vessel be unable to rise to the surface, the crew can retire to the apparatus and indicate the locality of the vessel by means of a cable. It is provided with a searchlight, rocket, telephone, alarm and signal bell. The apparatus is constructed so as to give easy exit and is fitted up with cupboards containing food and clothing and first-aid accessories. Considerable attention is being directed towards this invention by the British Admiralty. The exhibit," the report continued "should contain much to interest all patrons of the Links Market".

This rather macabre side-stall exhibited photographs of the railway disaster at Burntisland which happened a few days before the 1914 Market.
(Fife Council Libraries)

The boxing booths were perennial favourites. One of the legendary boxing figures around the early 1900s was Jimmy Lavin, known as 'the hero of a hundred fights' or 'Professor of the Fistic Arts' as the flowery Edwardian phrases had it. The *Fife Free Press* of around the same time reported that a photographer's studio had set up next to the boxing booth, "where persons

could have their portraits taken before they went into the sparring booths, so that they might be able to know what like they once were".

The booths always drew crowds of spectators. "Patterson and Stewart, they had the boxing booths; they paraded the boxers out on a platform and shouted out 'Is there anyone from the audience will challenge this one?'" recalled John Crichton. "If anyone volunteered, they threw them a pair of boxing gloves. The audience paid to get into the tent to watch, it was all enclosed, and you waited long enough till they got the tent filled up." Many people remembered one local contender, Arthur 'Tiny' Clephane, with great affection. Brought up in the Links area, he was a challenger from a very young age before going on to become a booth boxer, where his considerable height was a great advantage.

Local man Alex McGrow remembered the year that he took part in one of the boxing booths when he was a teenager in 1963. "I was an amateur welterweight with Kinghorn Boxing Club, and I saw one of the travelling boxers building up his booth," he said. "We got chatting, and he suggested that I earned an easy £3 by challenging him from the crowd. At that time I was earning £7 a week as an 18 year-old clerk in a local linen factory, so this was big money to me. I knew that as an amateur, I'd be banned if anyone in authority knew I was doing this, but money talked. We knocked lumps out of each other for three rounds, and the crowd loved it. He went round the crowd with a hat to collect for 'the boxers' benevolent fund' and collected over £3 in loose change.

"The next day one of the other boxers said that had been a great fight, and suggested that I challenge every night and 'make it look good' without anyone getting hurt. I stood in the crowd

Ron Taylor's Boxing Booth was one of several boxing pavilions which drew huge crowds each year. Volunteers in the audience challenged the professionals, and this 1964 photograph shows someone with his hand up ready to take part.
(Fife Council Libraries)

Advert for Stewart's Boxing Booth in the *Fife Free Press* of 1930.

NOTICE.

J. STEWART'S
HIGH · CLASS BOXING PAVILION
Will visit the
LINKS MARKET, 17th, 18th and 19th April,
At WEST END
With a School of Scientific BOXERS.

SPECIAL Contests will be held Each Evening. The Proprietor invites all comers, and will give prizes in Money to anyone who stands the limited number of rounds with any member of the staff. This concern is practically new this year, and is partly seated out, and is acknowledged to be the best travelling in Great Britain.

Prices Moderate.

and when he asked for challengers, I would go forward to get things going. The first couple of bouts were for real and after that it looked good—but we were actually just playing and nobody got hurt.

"Then I was asked to be a booth fighter and take challenges from the crowd—sometimes one or two of my friends would challenge me and we made it look real with a lot of fast action. If the crowd had known that their half-crown entry money was spent to watch a fix, they would have probably ripped us all and the tent to bits. Most of the guys that came out of the crowd to challenge weren't boxers, they were just brawlers. They got £1 a round, £3 if they lasted three rounds. If someone wasn't very good, you would just carry them. I dealt with them quite gently because I was getting my money anyhow, but the real fighters couldn't afford to do that because it was their bread and butter. They would be travelling round, Kirkcaldy one week, Dundee or Perth the next. At the end of the week I spent my money on a made-to-measure suit in a green and black check and 14" bottoms from Burtons!"

Ron Taylor of Cardiff came to the 1964 Market, presenting his boxing and wrestling 'school of champions' for the first time in Scotland. He was popularly known as the carnival boxing king, and once boxed in the booth which he later took over. "I remember Taylor had a wrestler, a monster of a guy who must have been about 6'6"," said Alex McGrow. "He just rolled the challengers over and really he was quite gentle with them, but it looked impressive."

One man in his eighties remembered the booths from before the war. "When a local man would step forward to challenge, the professional boxers didn't like it if he was too good. They would sometimes not keep to the Marquess of Queensberry rules, and more than once there would be a bit of a riot in the crowd when this happened and the police would have to come along."

Traders, who travelled round with their market stalls but who were not showmen, set out their wares in rows at the west end of the Prom and were very much in evidence until the 1960s. "You always bought a balloon or a birler or a hat and sword for the kids. There were squeaky toys, or a puggy—a monkey attached to a stick with elastic. And the jewellery stalls were lovely—you could

Davie Clark at his shooting stall around 1955 with his wife Amy (whose father 'Spider' Stewart had a boxing booth) and (background) Cissie Dick.
(William Dalgleish)

Marie, Sally and Frances Pinder with their side show of a snake act which also included a 21 foot boa constrictor.
(Edwin Pinder)

get heart-shaped badges and they used a thin wire to put your name on it."

"There were always a lot of stalls at the far end at the bus garage and were very popular," said another man. "They would always have a huge audience round about them—not many people actually bought anything but they all enjoyed listening to the patter. We used to go a walk along the prom to the far end where the traders' stalls were. They had curtains, towels, household stuff, cutlery, china, they would tell you the price and say 'what will you give me for this?' You used to get some good bargains."

Not everyone agreed. "I remember when I was a teenager in the late thirties, being attracted to a stall decorated with glittering ornaments, with an old gramophone, wound by hand, playing *Roses of Picardy*," said one local woman. "The stall holder held up a tea-set with very pink roses and very gold leaves, and called out 'Come on now ladies, who'll buy the last three tickets for the genuine Roses of Picardy china? Thank you, ladies, you all have lucky faces!' The number on my ticket was 177 and that was the winning one. Because the box was heavy to carry, he suggested I left it with him and collected it later. After we had gone round all the attractions, I went back for my china and carried the box home on the bus. I lifted the lid to show off my treasure to the family; but in amongst the curly straw were six plain white cups, saucers and plates. It taught me the hard way to be less trusting, but it never spoiled the memories of the day."

Another local man remembered the street traders to his cost. "I remember buying a pair of nylon stockings for my mother for half a crown, and when she opened up the packet when I got home, there were no toes in them. By the time I got back to the Prom, the chap was long gone. You could either get a bargain or a load of rubbish. One of the stall holders would hold up a bundle of towels, tea towels and pillow cases, and say 'Who'll give me £1 for this lot?' Once he had a dozen customers all with their hands up, he would say 'I'm not even going to charge you £1, I'll give it to you for ten shillings.' Of course that was to draw the crowds."

Pinder's Royal No 1 Circus in 1952 shows Elizabeth and Amelia Pinder at the entrance drawing in the crowds, with Amelia's husband, Koko the Clown.
(Fife Council Libraries)

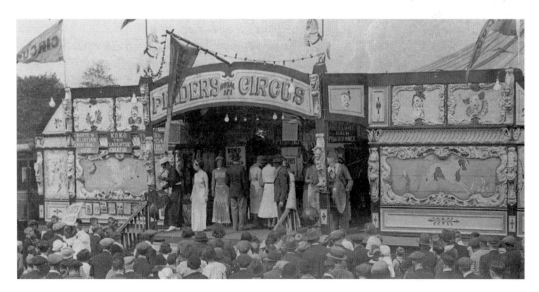

**Advert for Pinder's
Royal Circus in the
Fife Free Press of
1915**

'Freak' shows are now things of the past, and even then some people found them uncomfortable viewing. "Shows like the bearded lady and these tiny people—I felt at the time it wasn't right to treat them like that."

To others however they were a source of curiosity and amazement to many onlookers. "The things I liked best were the shows, like the smallest lady in the world," recalled Helen Main. "She was tiny, she was about the size my four year-old grand-daughter is now, and she had her own little house with all the tiny wee things that a little lady would have, her chairs and table. It was big enough for her to go into it, though I didn't know whether or not she slept in it. There was a barrier round it so we could walk round and look in.

"This was well before the war, maybe in the 1930s, and one thing I never forgot was the headless lady. You went in and this lovely young lady was there on the stage and she wore a one-piece green bathing suit—only she had no head. I was only young, and I found that very interesting because I couldn't understand where her head was. There were tubes at her back and they were supposed to keep her alive; but you didn't get to walk around her.

"Then there was the world's tallest man, but after you had paid to get in, here it was a skeleton in a coffin. He was very tall I suppose, but I found that a wee bit disappointing."

Local man Derry Sinclair, who has attended the Market for around sixty years, commented: "You wouldn't get that type of show now, but at the time they didn't bother me—it was just other things to see, and how else could they make a living? The only one I remember now was the Tallest Man, he must have been about 7'3", a Scotsman in a kilt. You could get your photo taken standing beside him which I did, and he thanked me afterwards because people wouldn't come forward. There were also strip shows and exotic

**Pinder's Royal No 1
Circus at its
traditional stance in
the Basin in 1952. The
front of the show
included the family's
living wagons on each
side of the centre
stage. Koko the Clown
is pictured drumming
up business.**
(Fife Council Libraries)

dancers, with a man with a moustache standing outside shouting 'Come in, Come in'!"

At one time there were two Pinder's circuses standing side by side in their traditional place at the Basin. Edwin Ord Pinder's Royal No. One Circus appeared there for many years; he proudly displayed the 'Royal' tag after being commanded to perform at Balmoral on three occasions between 1871 and 1899. One such appearance came when the circus was at Braemar and a letter was delivered from Queen Victoria requesting them to come to Balmoral—but not to bring the lions.

"Pinder's Royal Circus came, and sometimes it was Pinder's Australian Circus or Pinder's South African circus," said John Crichton. "It was famous; they used to parade along the High Street with a lion (a very old one) in a cage, elephants, clowns, horses, and ladies dressed up in spangles."

Or as another local put it: "At the top end was Pinder's Royal Circus, which no matter when you went was always 'just about to commence.' We preferred to watch the free show out front. Koko and Pepe the clowns tossed Indian clubs, the Pinder sisters twirled parasols, strong-men lifted dumbbells, there were drums and cymbals, and the ringmaster in his top hat and tails called out the programme and the admission prices."

The circus was set up in an ingenious way, although this was not always apparent to bystanders. "The family's living wagons formed the two side sections of the entrance to the circus. The top and bottom shutters folded on to the side and roof to protect the artwork, and also to give an efficient form of storage on the road," said Edwin Pinder. "The customers entered the show by walking over the disguised platform of an Albion lorry, although most people wouldn't realise that. Originally there would be a fairground organ at the front, and there was a large parading platform on the front where the performers came out to attract people into the show. The platform as well as the vestibule was built up from scratch and hooked to the wagons on each side."

Philip Paris recalled Pinder's circus well, with its entrance of steps and decorated panels between the wagons. "Although it looked like one big circus, when you walked up the stairs and into the circus, you were actually walking between the caravans. I remember when I was very young, looking in one of the caravan windows as I passed and saw Koko putting his clown outfit on!"

A circus elephant posed obligingly beside a local road-sweeper.
(Fife Council Museums: Kirkcaldy Museum and Art Gallery)

The big top itself was between 85 ft and 100 ft across, including guy ropes, with the smaller form used at the Market as space was restricted. "We used green canvas, laced up in four places, for the big top as it was less likely than other colours to rot or fade with the sun," said Edwin Pinder. "Boscoe the elephant used to tow the living wagons between the towns where the circus stopped. He died at the age of 60, and by that time he must have walked the equivalent of Land's End to John o' Groats and back a couple of times."

Another member of the circus family, the late Carl Pinder, was a talented artist who not only decorated the front boards of the rides but also drew and painted the fairgrounds which were exhibited in art galleries throughout the country. He was also a member of the Scottish showmen's band in the 1960s called 'Carl and the Comets' in which he played the drums. "My father Ernie Wilmot played accordion in the band and so did George Robert Hanley," said Hayley Paris, "and my uncle Ritchie Wilmot played guitar. They played at our annual function, Showland's Own Get-Together, which is held as a treat for the older folk in showmen's families. Although the band has wound up now, the function is still held—in fact it celebrated its fiftieth anniversary in 2003—with a meal, a cabaret and a dance band."

One local recalled: "Before Bingo came along, there were sideshows called Spinners, which were round stalls packed with prizes all stacked up. There was a big board with numbers and flashing lights and a spinner in the centre of it, which according to the showman's preference was an aeroplane, a horse or a rocket. The spinner stopped at a number and if you had the corresponding ticket, you got the prize.

"The fairground fairings were gingerbread and pan drops which always seemed to be larger than others and which had a clove in the middle. As a kid, I always remember going home with a sugar mouse, but as you got older and began to realise there weren't just boys around, you started buying sugar hearts instead. And the Market chips used to taste better than any other on earth, they had a far superior taste to the shop ones. Folk bought chips down the Market when they wouldn't have been seen dead buying them anywhere else."

Some of the attractions were summed up by Jock Mackie, who added poetry to his skills of sweetie-making:

Barnum and Bailey's Circus procession in 1902 in Kirkcaldy High Street. This was bound for one of the town's parks and shows the crowds which were drawn by a circus parade through the town.
(Fife Council Museums: Kirkcaldy Museum and Art Gallery)

Big moothed men and games o' chance
Dark-skinned girls in native dance
Fat ladies, dwarfs and monster rats,
Bows an' arrows, Cowboy hats.
Helter-skelter, Chair o' planes,
Roonaboots tae please the weans;
Bingo stalls, coconut shies
Great big wheels up tae the skies.
Young boys in the strip-tease tent—
Let's hope their mithers never kent.
Chip cairts, hot-dogs, toffee apples
Tae please a' kinds o' different thrapples.
Sugar hearts an' gingerbreid,
Showmen's dugs that need a feed.

The Wall of Death made its first appearance in the early 1930s, with its bowl-shaped wooden structure round which motor cyclists hurtled with split-second timing watched by the audience from the top. Stuntmen with names like Easy Jack Lancaster, Speedy Sedgwick, Fearless Violet and Cyclone Hogan kept the crowds on the edge of their seats as they carried out their well-rehearsed tricks. Lancaster would take both hands off his machine to wave to the crowds, and then take his female partner on to the handlebars of his bike—blindfold. Small wonder then that he came to grief when his tyre burst during his act; but despite a stitched chin, bandages and a bad limp, he returned to his act next day, with a placard from the *Dundee Courier* announcing his accident hanging at the entrance to the show.

"The crowds used to love the Wall of Death," said one local man. "The motor bikes would start on ground level and the crowd would go in and sit on the top of this circular wooden shell in circles of tiered seats. The motor bikes kept going round and round and up and up—you had a head like three at the end of it, because of the fumes of the exhausts which got trapped inside."

"Then there was the Globe of Death, which was a big lattice metal globe, like a ball with a door in it," recalled Tom Carmichael, who was born and brought up in the Links. "It had small motor cycles which would start going round and round and then the girl used to go on pillion in the back, up and down and round about like the ones on the Wall of Death."

Amusement arcades with coin-operated games have been part of the Market for generations. "Our family have had the same type of arcade stalls since the late 1900s, and at one time my father used to build machines and sell them to other showmen," said Philip Paris. "Some games have changed with fashions—from the mid-1970s until fairly recently, TV-type video games were all the rage. Then all the youngsters started to get Playstations so that died out. But some games like push the coins, or 'penny falls', are still as popular as ever although they're now operated by ten-pence pieces rather than pennies."

Chapter 4
Local memories

"The Market was part of tradition, it had to come every year," said Myra Bell, who was born and brought up in Links Street. "We used to go down every night and we walked home from school that way—you always had to walk down and see it. We were inundated with friends and relations who all came to the house for coffee and to use your toilet. Some days you couldn't get down to the market till 10 p.m. because of all the visitors, and then the next invasion would arrive—but my mother enjoyed it. My granny's cousins lived at the foot of Buchanan Street and she had a roundabout right outside her window, but they loved it. Everyone gave you a penny, and if you were lucky you got sixpence. That was just after the war, when most rides were fourpence, and sixpence on the Saturday.

"I can always remember on Easter Sunday in the Fifties when the Market was there but not open, you could see the kids from the show families going from caravan to caravan picking up their Easter eggs. The wee girls were beautifully dressed, very very expensive dresses which must have cost a fortune," she recalled, still wistfully remembering the wonder of these dresses when most girls in post-war Kirkcaldy were wearing serviceable skirts and hand-knitted cardigans.

"It was a mark in time, like Christmas," agreed her husband Jim Bell. "When it started up again after the war, there were no new rides as they had all just been brought out again after being in storage. Then the Whip came in—it was an oval shape driven by a cable on the inside with trolleys attached to seat four people. When they turned round at the ends, they were whipped round quickly and we all thought that was amazing. Then the new stuff all followed, like the Rotor where you stuck to the wall and the Cyclone. There was the Caterpillar, basically like the Speedway only it had a green cover over the carriages and gave a short period of privacy!

"There were very many more traders then—you could spend a whole evening just going through the traders' stalls. I remember there was a man selling nylons out of the back of a van on Volunteers' Green just after the war. Rationing was

A group of local mothers strolled along the Prom with their children in the early 1950s in the post-war style of prams.
(Don Swanson)

still on, and he came with all these boxes and boxes of nylons. They turned out to be just nylon-coloured stockings and not even particularly well made. The ladies of the Links got a bit irate and grabbed hold of him, and he ended up in the sea."

Nancy Brodie knows the Market better than most local people, having lived for more than forty years in a house which has seen many Markets come and go; it was built in the days before the Prom was made up and its original postal address was Sands Road. "Our family love the Market—all the people who were born and bred here like the Market; all the complaints come from the incomers! It's only here for a week in the year and we have double glazing so the noise doesn't bother us much; the way the wind blows it goes over the top of our house to the streets behind.

"When the Market shuts down at night it's so quiet, just a deathly hush— much quieter than it is normally because we're used to the background sound of traffic going along the Prom all the time. It doesn't really disturb our sleep because it's closing down at bedtime anyway, and if you're at the back of the house with the door shut you wouldn't know it was even going on.

"The caravans used to be all along the sea wall, interspersed between the roundabouts and shows, and at one time we had one right underneath us— you could have stepped out of the window on to its roof. We were never bothered by them, and in fact before the new houses were built, I used to say it was the only week in the year when I had neighbours. Now we just have the lorries which have to be three feet away from the door for fire

All aboard for Kaye and Swallow's children's ride in 1958.
(National Fairground Archive)

precautions. It was a big change when the caravans were moved. Some of the showmen give me their mobile phone numbers for security, so if I see anything suspicious from my window I can let them know."

Her late husband John, who followed his father and grandfather in the family leather business in Links Street, had great enthusiasm for the event. "John was a great Market man—he used to walk through it every day when the shop was closed for lunch," Nancy Brodie said. "White's Waltzer was across from the house, and John could tell whether it was in exactly the same place as the previous year, or whether it had moved so many feet the other way. He used to time the rides on the Waltzer and count how many folk went on it, and then worked out exactly how much money they had made! You could see old Granny White going every night until she was in her nineties to collect the drawings from the Waltzer. We could watch them putting the prices up for Fridays and Saturdays, or reduce them if there weren't very many people about.

"People who lived further up the town could always pretend to their children that the market was away, but we couldn't do that when our two children were young as it was right outside the window. Instead, we used to ration out their money so that when it was finished, that was it. Mr Swallow stood at the bottom of Bute Wynd with his children's roundabout, and if it was quiet he used to tell me to put our kids on the roundabout because it would draw more on, so they got a lot of free rides. Mr Newton had a side-stall in the early 1970s where you could win a goldfish, and at the end of the week he would give our children all the goldfish that were left over.

You could pay to have your photograph taken with a well-dressed monkey in 1965 . . .
(Dryna Innes)

"You used to see vans coming from the Border mills with sweaters and tweeds to sell to the show families before the Market opened to the public. There were wholesale vans too with soft toys and other things for prizes, which the showmen would buy in quantity for their stalls. The casual workers used to have their own small caravans and we would see them going off to the swimming baths for a wash!

"When I was married first, the roundabouts were built up on old lemonade boxes as their base—of course that would never happen now, but it never caused any accidents."

She too finds her house suddenly very popular with friends and relations when the Market is here. "It must have about the best view in town. We used to have our tea on a card table at the window so we could watch everything that was going on while we were eating. It used to stay open till midnight on the Saturday, when it was always packed; the policeman would start at the other end and tell the Market people to shut the rides down, but as soon as he had moved on they would open up again! One year my family were here until quarter to one and it still wasn't shut. We had a Special Constable who was always down on site, but we never saw any trouble."

All the local children looked forward to the Market for weeks, and used to be let off school early on the Friday afternoon. For youngsters, gathering together the necessary spending money beforehand could be quite a challenge. "Every time we got a penny we would run down the Market. We would save up for weeks, run messages for a penny, and sell 'jeely jars'. You were paid threepence for clearing the weeds out of the church grounds and you visited all your relatives beforehand in the hope of getting a Market penny."

. . . or to sit on a stuffed tiger
(Sheena Graham)

"You saved up all your rags and old woollens for months and you asked all your aunties to keep theirs for you. Then you carried all these bags of rags up to Denburn to sell them to 'Pud' Paterson, because he gave you the best prices," said a woman who lived in Cowan Street in the late 50s and early 60s. "Some of the boys used to collect scrap metal like old bits of drainpipes, put that all in a barrow and wheel it up to Lennie the scrap merchant.

"The great thing then was that you had to wear a cowboy hat, that was the fashion. We used to steam it from one year to another, which saved you having to buy another one and that left more money for going on the Waltzers. The only thing was that each year your hat got smaller and smaller. You didn't wear a jacket because that would cramp your style, you had to wear a big sweater."

Another woman who was brought up in Links Street said: "You always got dressed up to go because you never knew who you would meet. If you got a fellow to take you to the Market on Saturday night, that was really something, especially if you were in a group of six or eight."

The distinctive noise and smell of the Market was part of the whole event. "When I was a teenager, it was all such an excitement and just such a buzz," said Dryna Innes. "It was the smell of the heat off the big machines, the diesel generators, the hot dogs and sugar smell of the candy floss, mixed up with the sea air and the music. You didn't really get hot dogs anywhere else then because they didn't have outdoor eating places, there were no burger stands. It was such a unique experience because you didn't have take-away food apart from fish and chips. It was always warm when you went on to the decking around the rides especially the Waltzers, which must have come from the heat off the machinery. You met up with everyone and you bumped into people that you hadn't seen for months or years.

Bill Chalmers (left), Albert Marsh and (right) David McIlravie having a spin on the Waltzers in 1947.
(Albert Marsh)

"I remember standing at the bus stop at Buckhaven where I lived, watching as bus after bus passed, and you couldn't get on because they were jam packed with folk going to the Market in the evening. They were all double-deckers, packed

Evans' Waltzer ready for action at the 1958 Market.
(National Fairground Archive)

with people both upstairs and downstairs. You were lucky if you got on a bus, and sometimes you had to go to Leven to get on at the bus station."

Some of the prizes at the sideshows were ornaments such as dogs, cats, rabbits and plaques with crinoline ladies on them, made out of soft chalk. They broke easily, and were put to a new use chalking out the 'pauldy beds' (the universal street game known outside Fife as hopscotch or peever). "You would see the bairns chalking the pauldy beds, they were using the legs broken off the chalk alsations."

The circuses had their own traditional place at the far end of the Prom in the basin. "Pinder's Circus put out a challenge in 1930 and asked if anyone would like to go into the cage with the lions. My mother, Janet Dewar, decided she would have a go, and she went into the cage," said Wendy Younger. "The ringmaster walked round the edges and the lions were in another corner, I believe there were four of them. She had to walk right round the four corners of the cage, being protected by the ringmaster. She got half a crown and a brooch in the shape of a shield with her initials and the date on it, and topped by a lion. She was always so proud of that brooch.

"My older sister as a wee girl had watched her walk inside the lions' cage, and when she got married she wore it pinned on her wedding suit, just to remember our mum.

"We stayed friendly with the Pinders and they would ask us into their caravan—they expected us to be down there and looked out for us. My sister still went down to see them once they had stopped the big circus and just had a little zoo and dogs that did tricks, maybe around the 1950s. She made clothes for the performing dogs—they would play *Sweet Little Alice Blue Gown*, and the dog would wear a little blue gown which my sister had made."

For one local woman of 80, the highlight of the Market was the sideshows. "When I was young, it was just magic to me. Because we lived in Chapel, which was the country then, I wasn't allowed to go by myself. I used to watch my big brothers and sisters going to the Market and coming back with fancy boxes of chocolates with ribbons, and coconuts. Then when I was about 12, I got to go with my mother and we would go round all the sideshows.

"They had all these stalls with things like china and china ornaments; you bought a pink or a green ticket and if you were lucky, you won a prize. My mother got a ticket and the man came up and asked me to pick out the winning one, and I pulled my own ticket out! I got this great big beautiful fluffy white dog—it was lovely, not like the cheap things you see now. It was

Koko the Clown (Harry Salvona) in Pinder's circus ring with his dog and goat act.
(Edwin Pinder)

too good to play with, and my mother put it on her couch as an ornament when we got home. Another time the man asked me to pull out the winning ticket, and it happened again—and I got a china half tea-set with roses on it and gold round the edges. Twice that happened! and I've never won anything since.

"There were dancing girls in fancy clothes who came out on the stage in front of the circus and other shows, which I suppose was to draw you in. I liked to see that because you didn't need to go in to enjoy watching them."

Her husband added some of his own memories. "Before the war, there was a game for the youngsters which was called 'Pull the Old Man's Whiskers', and it was a big painted face with strings coming out of the mouth. Each string was attached to a prize at the back of the stall. You paid your ha'penny or whatever, and got a string and pulled on it for your prize—everyone got a prize, but you just hoped you got one of the really good ones. It would be a trinket or a wee toy, and you would see a wee tray coming up and your prize would be on it.

"There were wee children's habby-horses, and the men would wind it round and round with a handle, before electricity came along.

"I used to like watching the steam engines which did the whole show—they pulled the wagons and they had a dynamo in front that would keep the lights going for the caravans and give the power for the rides. They were polished even underneath the canopy, polished brass, the wheels were painted and they had strings of bulbs all lit up round them—they were beautiful things. The showmen took a real pride in them and looked after them very well.

Mothers look on as youngsters take a spin in Thomas's juvenile ride in 1958.
(National Fairground Archive)

"The steam engines would stand in the road behind the caravans; they would sit there all the time with big barrels of water for the engine. I used to sit in a corner and watch them building up the Chair o' planes. They would put three pieces of wood underneath to balance it and then the steam engine would lift up a big steel rod into position and the men would build the Chair o' planes round it.

"I was in digs in Links Street at one time, and Graham's Steamboats were right outside my window. He only had four records which he used to play over and over again all night!

"Then there were the acts that followed the shows around, like the strong man act. They tied the man up in chains and put a big stone on top of his chest, and asked if anyone from the crowd could come and break the stone with a hammer. They broke it all the time and then the boy would just sit up, nothing wrong with him. Another one was all chained up and he would have to get himself out of the chains. You didn't pay to get in to see them, but there was a collection 'in case they didn't survive'!"

Another local man said: "There were lots of 'quacks' who came with patent medicines which were guaranteed to cure anything, and I remember there was one who would offer to cure cataracts by licking it off your eye. Then there were girlie shows where the girls danced in feathers and goose pimples. One of the sideshows was advertised as the Lady with the Bare Behind—she turned out to be holding a teddy bear against her fully covered bottom, a great disappointment for teenage boys!"

Some of the 'freak' shows survived until the 1960s. "I remember George, the Gentle Giant. You were allowed to go up and take his hand, and his hands were soft and gentle even though they were huge."

The coconut shies played a bit part in one Dysart woman's memories. "We used to go down on the Saturday afternoon and we just had to win a coconut," she said. "Once you got one, you asked your father to give it a bash and made two holes in it—one for the air to come out and the other to let the milk out. We drank the milk and then on the Sunday afternoon, we made coconut tablet from the inside.

"On the Saturday afternoon, you would see the girls from the factories in their curlers and headscarves, and in the evening they were there again but with their hair all brushed out."

A local man added: "There were often a lot of workers from Nairn's and Barry's down on the Thursday night, as the linoleum workers got paid then so they had money before the other workers who often didn't get their pay packets until Saturday."

"When I served my apprenticeship at Bryce's foundry in Dunnikier Road in the 1930s, we did a lot of work on the showmen's engines," said Tom Carmichael. "They would need them repaired or maintained, and I was fine and wee so I used to get right in the firebox working away to clean out the boilers."

Alex Lafferty had his own associations with the Market, being Commandant of St Andrew's Ambulance Corps from 1982 until he retired twenty years later. "We are all trained volunteers and attend every Market, walking from end to end and then back again to be on hand in case there are any accidents or incidents which need First Aid," he said. "When I was Commandant, I tried to get a team of up to 20 people working in shifts. I sent them out in pairs, so that if there was a patient needing attention, one would stay there while the other contacted a policeman. Our base is in the Philp Hall and we also have a mobile First Aid post at Nicol Street. Over the years we have had to attend to all kinds of incidents, from children's minor accidents to more major things; one of the most common calls for attention is someone having an epileptic fit which is brought on by the lights and the music.

Racing off to put out a fire was a serious business in the early 1950s.
(Dryna Innes)

Concentration on the faces of local young-sters as they tried their hands at a game of skill in the 1950s.
(Robert Foster)

"When you walked through so often in your uniform, all the Market people got to know you. You weren't allowed to go on the machinery or the rides when you were on duty, but if you wanted a wee shot at the funfair you could tell your CO, sign off for half an hour, and enjoy yourself for a wee while without breaking any regulations. I remember in the 1950s when they had the boxing booths—we sometimes had to give the challengers smelling salts or splash water on their faces. I used to think it was a very sore way to earn £3. One of the regular challengers, I think we carried him out more times on a stretcher than he walked out.

"When I first started, you had to carry a casualty on a stretcher the full length of the Prom back to the Philp Hall. Now the side streets leading up to the Links are used as escape routes so that if an ambulance is needed, it can come straight down to the exact section of the ground where they are needed. I still do the Market to help out, I enjoy it."

Free tickets (Codona's, late 1960s, Kirkcaldy Links Market, 1990s) were handed round to visitors.
(Alan Ingram)

Derry Sinclair has always had a great fascination for the Market. "I can remember sitting on our stairs as a little boy when I was about four, just before the War, counting my money to take to Rolling the Pennies," he said. "When I was a bit older I would sit on the walls at the Links watching all the different types of trucks coming in, lorries with trailers pulling all the rides At that time, that was as exciting to me as the Market itself—now of course they're specialised trucks so you can't see what's in them. I remember one year, probably in the 1950s, seeing one big truck going down Commercial Street on the way to the Market. It tried to go round the corner towards Factory Road and one of the central trailers which carried the Waltzer or Speedway broke away and crashed right through the Store window in Commercial Street.

"For many years there really weren't new attractions—they maybe modified them slightly but it was basically Waltzers, Speedway, Dodgems, Chair o' planes, Big Wheel, that sort of thing. There were the Tin Boxes, like a Big Wheel, and electric cars which you drove round a big track—a bit like Dodgems but you weren't supposed to bump into each other. Dan Taylor from Kirkcaldy had the Whip, although that's finished now. I'm amazed at the amount of new equipment that has appeared over the last five years or so, you just didn't get that before. I still enjoy going to see the Market; I enjoy seeing the people and the kids and I take photos to record the scene.

"I remember when the habby horses were still driven by steam, but I think the last steam-driven rides were the Steamboats—they were great. There were two big carriages that you could get a load of people in, maybe about 30 at a time. There were four or five lines of seats going straight across, and there were ropes to hang on to at the back and at both sides. It was like a massive swing, it went right up and down the other side and your stomach just left you; they were possibly the most exciting ride there was then.

"There were stalls at the very beginning of the Market near Volunteers' Green selling coconuts in case you didn't win one; and Jock Mackie sold his sugar hearts there too."

The traditional sugar hearts have special memories for Peter Saunders, whose great-grandfather was 'Paurley' Kidd who had a baker and confectioners' business in the Gallatown area of Kirkcaldy. "He used to go to the Market with a confectionery stall, and my grandmother passed on his recipe to my parents who had a small stall selling Curly Andrews and sugar hearts during the Depression. They were struggling for money, every copper was a captive," Peter Saunders said. "My parents made sugar hearts in our kitchen in their spare time in the winter when they could afford to buy sugar. They could be stored for maybe three months as long as they were dried, so my father would store them in orange boxes and keep them covered until it was time for the Market. My grandmother gave them a secret ingredient to drop in when the sugar was boiling at a certain temperature, to make the sugar hearts fluff up—it wasn't bicarbonate of soda, that just made them hard. They took a drop or two of the mixture and put it on a cold saucer, and when it cracked they knew it was ready for pouring into the metal heart-shaped moulds. I used to rub cooking fat into the moulds to stop them sticking, and I got my fingers burnt a few times trying to get them turned out quickly. Some were white and some were coloured pink using a drop or two of cochineal. They sold for a penny and twopence, and threepence for the big ones.

J. & A. KIDD
Rosslyn Confectionery Works
KIRKCALDY

Manufacturers of High-Class Boilings, Toffees, Rocks, &c.

We Specially Recommend Our Puff Toffee.

1924 advertisement in the Kirkcaldy Directory for J & A Kidd, confectioners who made sugar hearts and gingerbread for the Market.

"They also made Curly Andrews which were hard-boiled sweets, some were coated almonds or cloves and some pure sugar. My grandmother, who had worked in her father's boiling shop at the Gallatown, also showed us how to make cartons like a tube which you filled with Curly Andrews and sealed with sealing wax, and I helped with that. They made gingerbread too, square and flat and wrapped in silver paper for Market fairings.

"My father knew several of the showmen, such as Wattie Wilmot who had the Jumpers or Gallopers, and as a child I used to get on the Jumpers for free! He had the Cakewalk too, and I remember my mother trying to catch me on the moving platform to take me home while Wattie was watching and laughing. Then there was Harry Knowles, who had a small children's roundabout which turned round with a handle like a mangle, Swingboats or 'jow' boats where you pulled the ropes, and Chair o' planes. He was one of the first to have petrol to run the Dodgem cars and he got a joiner from Thornton to make a track for them. He let me go on them to try them out before they opened, so that all the other kids could see them and of course when they started up, they were there with their threepence or sixpence. Bob Lovett was good at helping my parents out; because their sweet stall had no electricity, he ran a wire from his generator and a couple of bulbs to light up the stall. I used to manage Mrs Lovett's Bingo stall for her in later years when she wasn't so well."

A showmen's football team in the 1950s along with their supporters.
(Philip Paris)

For many years, there was an annual football match played in Stark's Park with a team from Fife Police playing the Showmen, with proceeds going to charity—followed by a dance that evening in the Raith Ballroom. "The match was a regular event which went on until at least

1968, which is the last mention of it in Raith Rovers' Minutes, but there may well have been the occasional fixture going on into the early 1970s," said football historian John Litster. "It wasn't played every year; in 1947 for instance, when Chief Constable Peter Baldie asked the club for permission to use the ground, his request was turned down because of the state of the pitch after a very severe winter. I suspect that, as the years went on, the club would become reluctant to put on the fixture because of their other commitments. Once the club got its floodlights, for instance, there would be an increasing number of midweek and late League fixtures.

"When the fixture list is being drawn up before each season, Raith Rovers always ask for an away game on Market Saturday as a matter of course so as not to increase the already heavy traffic. There was one occasion however in 1960 when the semi-final replay of the Scottish Junior Cup between St Andrews United and Thornton Hibs was played at Stark's Park on that Saturday. Their original match had been played the week before, on 16 April, and ended up in a draw. The replay was scheduled for the next Saturday, as Rovers were playing away and the ground was available. It was the only time two Fife Junior teams have met in the Scottish Junior Cup, and the whole of Thornton turned out to support their team as well as a good proportion of fans from St Andrews. The gate was over 15,000 and the traffic congestion was absolute chaos.

"More recently, in 1997 when Raith Rovers were in the Premier League, someone slipped up when the fixtures were being drawn up and Raith had a home game arranged against Rangers on the Saturday of the Market. The police picked up on this a few months before the match, and postponed it until the following Wednesday—probably the only occasion that a Rangers game has been put off because of the Links Market!"

Nancy Brodie remembered one of the charity matches for more personal reasons. "They used to have the match the night before the Market opened, and the Provost's wife kicked off," she recalled. "Provost Nicholson's wife preferred not to do it, so as my husband was a senior magistrate, I was asked if I would do it, so I did—even though I was pregnant at the time!"

One local couple have particularly happy memories of the Market Saturday. Mary and Richard McGillvary got married then in 1949, and went for a spin on the Waltzer on their wedding day. Fifty years later, they were given VIP treatment by Fife Council, and were driven in the Council Convener's car down to the Prom to help in the official opening ceremony where they were presented with a giant greetings card to celebrate their Golden Wedding.

"We lived in the Links and my mother used to try to stop me going down to the Market all the time but of course we always did," said Edith Williamson. "I had very fair hair then, and all the dust from the shows got caught up in it so my mother took one look at me when I came back and knew where I'd been. We grew up with it; we went to Pinder's circus, the first one I'd been to, and I saw the woman doing tricks on the horse. People always lost a lot of coins when they did rolling the pennies, so after the Market went away, we would go and look where the stall had been to collect any money that was dropped.

"My mother would be in the wash-house and the showmen would come and get hot water from her. That was when the caravans weren't so modern as they are now, and they had beautiful big water carriers made from brass."

Local people living in the Links and on the Prom itself were involved in some of the day to day life of the showmen's families. "The caravans were parked right up to the house windows, packed together like herring in a barrel, and you had to keep your lights on all the time. There were no services laid on for the market people so they would plug into the electricity supply in our houses and gave us £1 per week, but it was better than having a noisy generator right outside your window. Market traders got passes to use the washing facilities of council tenants. Some of the stalls sold fresh flowers, and they were kept in our wash-houses so they could be kept watered until the stall was restocked.

"Most of the big roundabouts had their own engines, with standpipes put in to supply water. We used to go and ask if the engines needed water, and if they did, we would collect it and get a free ride from the owner. Links Market weather was a standing joke in the town, and there were a few times the high rides had to be taken down because of the wind. The showmen were often worried about the water coming over the sea wall, in case the caravans would be washed away."

Many of the youngsters who lived around the Links area were keen to help the showmen do odd jobs. "You would watch them drawing in, and go down when you were supposed to be at school and ask if they were needing any workers," said Mark Conroy. "I worked for Lovett who had the Helter-skelter—he would take the money on the ground and send me up the top, and every so often he would send me up a burger and a cup of tea. Later on I was on the Paratrooper, I loved helping to build that up, and then you got the first free rides on the Monday or Tuesday prior to opening—I suppose we were sort of guinea pigs.

"When I was about 13, I was a 'runner' for one of the traders who had the auction sales. He would put me in the middle of the crowd with some money, and he would call out 'Who's going to give me the first bid?' and that would be me. I would go forward and get this big beautiful tea service and run back through the crowd with it, so they could all see it. That built up a big crowd so they would all want to buy—but by that time, I had put the tea-set back in the trader's van.

"My grandmother lived in Invertiel Road and they used to do

A wooden living wagon of the 1920s with lace curtains and brass water carriers at the door.
(William Dalgleish)

the laundry for the Codonas. When my mother was still at school in the 1950s, she would go down with a wheelbarrow, collect the washing, bring it up to my granny who would wash it, press it and take it back. One of our neighbours used to take in some of the travelling workers for bed and breakfast.

"I used to run messages, maybe go for petrol for the generator, for Miss Pinder who had the Mini-zoo. She used to let me go and get her Shetland pony and help her brush it and groom it."

The decision to move the living wagons off the Esplanade was regretted by many local people as well as the showmen. "You would see just one bit of the caravan which was so attractive, and they seemed to have everything they needed. They kept them so well, and I would have loved to have gone inside," said one elderly lady wistfully. Another said: "I used to live in Forth View and we used to watch the Market people building up. One family had an old zinc bath outside the caravan and the men had to scrape off all the mud before they went in."

"Taking the living wagons off the Prom deprived the Market of a lot of the atmosphere," said a Kinghorn man. "I know it was for safety reasons, but the only fire I can recall was in a chip cart, and that didn't even belong to a showman. On Sundays, in the days before it was open, there used to be hundreds of people down during the day just to look at the caravans. If one of the show folk opened a caravan door, there was a crowd round trying to peer inside. Showmen were a world apart to Kirkcaldy people in those days; they could have come from Mars."

Another man went further. "Our mother warned us not to go near the caravans, because we would be taken away or locked up. It was quite a common myth even in the 1950s that the fairground people stole babies, so you weren't allowed to go down on your own."

"The Market was something you looked forward to all year, and when you saw the town workmen painting the white lines on the edge of the road, you knew it was nearly here," recalled Arnot Muir, who was born in Kinghorn and who has attended every Market for the past 70 years. "There used to be a white line a yard out from the kerb and no-one dared to build outwith that line. When Mr Hunter was Market Superintendent, I've seen him make showmen move machines because they were a couple of inches over the building line. When I was young, the fair used to

Time for a tea break (with china cups) in 1910 for Celie Clark (front), with Lizzie, Kate and Willie Clark sitting on the steps. Kate sent this postcard with the message "Just a pc to let you know I got home all right. Burtons aren't going to Anstruther yet so we are going to Elie for a week".
(William Dalgleish)

go right along to the bus office with a line of traders along the front of Volunteers' Green; most of the traders were from the Tiel Bridge up to the Fourways, not on the Prom at all. The bus paint shop, where their offices are now, had a big open yard where a lot of the living wagons parked with the traders' stalls round the pavement.

"It used to be the saying among the showmen that if you had a good Links Market, the rest of the year would look after itself. A good time at Kirkcaldy meant that paid the insurance, and the rest was basically found money. That's no longer the case because the expenses are now far too heavy. I was speaking to a showman this year, and he told me that his insurance had risen threefold, and he only has side stalls and juvenile rides.

"Looking back now, the machines never actually stopped on a Saturday, they just slowed down to let people off and on, or so it seemed to me as a youngster. I don't think the crowds are as big as they used to be. People used to refer to it as walking on the heads—it was absolutely solid with folk and you just shuffled along with the crowd."

The Market by night is still packed with visitors.
(Fife Council Libraries)

The Helter-skelter is still a firm favourite with children in the present day
(Ms Hall)

Hello ! Hello ! !
Kirkcaldy Speaking

Broadcast it.

Something Really New
HAS ARRIVED AT THE
LINKS MARKET FAIR GROUND
Foot of Buchanan Street.

CODONA BROTHERS Present their LATEST
NOVELTY RIDING MACHINE—
The WHIRLPOOL
and GLIDER WHEEL

First Visit Here. The Sensational Ride of the
Year. Don't Miss it ! Also their
New Golden Dragon Machine
with the Large Organ and Jazz Band
Playing the LATEST LONDON DANCE MUSIC.
Come and Listen to. "Little Nelly Kelly" and
Brighter London.
Look for the Name CODONA
at the foot of BUCHANAN ST.

The Codona Brothers advertised their Whirlpool Glider Wheel and Golden Dragon Machine in the *Fife Free Press* of 1924.

The Helter-skelter 'lighthouse' was introduced in 1908 and has been a firm favourite for the best part of a hundred years.
(Fife Council Libraries)

Chapter 5
Swings and Roundabouts

Each year it seems that the fairground rides get faster, more breathtaking and ever more sophisticated to suit the modern craving for thrills and speed. But amid all the up to the minute technology, some rides have been faithfully carried on or adapted from the days of steam.

One of the main landmarks in any fair, the Helter-skelter, was introduced to Kirkcaldy in 1908 when it was enthusiastically received. Although now it seems to have been around for ever, it was a novel enough attraction for the *Fife Free Press* of the day to explain how it operated for those who had not yet paid it a visit. "The Helter-skelter lighthouse rises to a height of about 50 feet. Passengers ascend a winding stair case to the top and, sitting on a mat, slide down to the bottom where they arrive with a bump." Perhaps its very simplicity has kept it an enduring favourite down the years.

Wilmot's Royal Patent Jumpers set up for action in the 1900s, with its hand carved horses and elaborately painted rounding boards at the top.
(Fife Council Museums: Kirkcaldy Museum and Art Gallery)

Another early favourite, still popular in the 1920s and 1930s and presumably named after the dance of the period, was the Cakewalk, remembered with great affection by many older residents. "The thing I mind is the Cakewalk, when you walked up stairs and you stood on this wooden platform and held on to handrails on the side," said one woman. "It was moving when you came on it, backwards and forwards. It seemed to have a shaking movement, it shook and shook up and down like a wave until you landed away at the other side. You were safe enough on it." It made its first appearance in Kirkcaldy in 1909 when the *Fife Free Press* commented: "The great attraction this year is the 'cake walk,' and it has the additional virtue of being quite as entertaining to the onlookers as to those who have paid their 2*d*. to walk over. The owner guaranteed it a perfect cure for indigestion or liver complaints, but advised all who were adorned with false hair to keep out of the way. The soundness of his advice was frequently manifested by some of the young women who were 'enjoying' the walk. Before they had completed the journey they had parted with both hat and hairpins, and in their extremity were embracing the attendants like long lost brothers."

One of the most basic rides is the roundabout—and whether it's called a carousel, merry go round, Gallopers, jumpers or hobby horses, its origins stretch back for centuries. One of the best known were Wilmot's Gallopers. Magnificent hand-painted and beautifully carved roundabout horses, they had a mechanism underneath so that they went up and down as well as round and round. The Gallopers stayed in the possession of the Wilmot family for the best part of a hundred years until the mid-1980s and still have a special place in the Market's history.

Many of Kirkcaldy's older residents remembered them. "They were like merry-go-round horses but there was a mechanism underneath to give them a galloping movement too," recalled John Crichton. "They had to come by rail, from Glasgow I think, and were brought down to the Prom from the station." Tom Carmichael said: "The Gallopers were pinned into each other two or three abreast on the ride, but to come down from the station there were all hooked up singly, one behind the other. I remember seeing that, I used to watch them coming in with the traction engine pulling them."

Another of Wilmot's rides was his set of Gondolas, advertised as "the largest and grandest roundabout now travelling. Illuminated nightly by Electricity. Come, see and hear the triumph of music and art." The steam engine in the centre of the ride turned the Venetian-style Gondolas and also powered the fairground organ, described on his poster as "Grand Parisian Gavioliphone—equal to a full military band, playing a choice selection of music comprising English, Irish, Scotch, continental and operatic selections at intervals." The exterior was decorated (according to contemporary accounts) with paintings of Queen Victoria, the Prince of Wales, Mr Gladstone, Lord Salisbury and Lord Rosebery, and a scenic painting of Charles I fleeing from Cromwell's army at the Battle of Naseby.

John Wilmot was one of the first to recognise the potential of steam driven roundabouts in the late nineteenth and early twentieth century. He was also said to be the first in Scotland to use electricity on his rides, and won a Golden Award at a Paris exhibition for his electrical equipment. Known fondly as 'Honest John', and a non-smoker and non-drinker, he and his wife Martha McIndoe had six sons and three daughters. The start of his fairground empire came after they married in 1865 when he was given the franchise to sell peanuts in Bostocks' menagerie; the copper scoop which measured how many peanuts were sold for a penny is still a family treasure today.

John Wilmot, founder of one of the best known fairground dynasties, is pictured (seated) around 1900 in front of his well decorated Molycroft wagon, together with sons Hughie (left) and Wattie (right) and grand-daughter Nancy.
(Fife Council Museums: Kirkcaldy Museum and Art Gallery)

As the popularity of steam roundabouts grew, so did the size of the fairs, and John Wilmot started to lease the whole ground at different venues. These astute moves, together with his expanding stable of Gallopers, Gondolas, Joywheel and racing cars made him a significant figure in the fairground world. He was Vice-President of the Showmen's Guild for many years; his generosity was well known and he was always one of the first to head the donations list each year at the Links Market. When he died in 1911, his funeral was attended by virtually every showground family in the country, and his descendents still play an active part in many fairs throughout Britain.

When the Market returned after the Second War, some rides were still manually operated— and some by the customers themselves. "I remember the Swingboats about 1950, and there were two people in a boat with a rope each—you did the pulling and you swung from side to side," said one woman. "I still recall the Steamboats after the war, when six of you sat on one side and six on the other, boys at one end and girls at the other.

Wilmot's Miniature Railway with its steam organ at the front is pictured around 1910. (Fife Council Museums: Kirkcaldy Museum and Art Gallery)

White's Speedway pictured in the 1950s. (Joe Richard White)

You held on to the ropes at the back or you'd have been flung right across—you started at the back but by the time they were finished you were sliding off.

"Then there was the Speedway, which had two rows of motor bikes with three bikes in a row in front of a carriage which was shaped like a dragon. You sat on the bikes or you could sit on a seat in carriages—which were bit like high-backed pews only fancier. As it went round, you all got squashed down to one side. The boys mostly sat on the bikes and sometimes they would change from one bike to another during the ride. Of course you weren't supposed to do that and they usually got into trouble.

"There was the Whip, the Doodlebugs which went up and down, and the Sky Diver which turned upside down and right over. It was almost like a Waltzer, but the carriages went into the middle and came in and back out, you swung round on the edge of the ride.

"I don't think I've missed a year, even now I still have a walk through even though I don't go on anything. The noise doesn't bother me, it's a funfair and you expect to have noise—the music makes it what it is. I think it's very well laid out now, much better organised with policemen up on the stands so that they can see over the heads of the crowd, and notices for the portable toilets."

One of the last steam-driven rides were the Steamboats, which first came to the Market in 1902 and lasted until the 1950s. "My brother was terrified of the Steamboats which stood near Bute Wynd, because of the noise the

A pair of Steamboats, Renown and Repulse, named after World War I battleships, are pictured in the 1920s. The carriages were driven by a steam engine (with its chimney in the middle of the ride) which also powered the organ. The sign on the right says '2d. a ride'.
(Fife Council Libraries)

Eddie Pinder's Haunted Castle in the 1970s. The front of the ride was built against the lorry's exterior with the entertainment inside.

(Arnot Muir)

White's Waltzer was sited directly opposite the Brodie family's window in 1976
(Nancy Brodie)

The late Carl Pinder, a talented artist, is pictured working on some of his fairground art in 1972
(Arnot Muir)

Posters advertising Anita, the World's Smallest Woman, and Titania, the Giantess, in the 1950s.
(Fife Council Museums: Kirkcaldy Museum and Art Gallery)

Choosing a lucky number can win a cuddly toy.
(Andrew Beveridge, Fife Council)

A tower of Winnie the Pooh bears could be won in this side-stall in 2002.
(Andrew Beveridge, Fife Council)

Brooch presented to Janet Dewar for walking inside the lions' cage at the circus.
(Wendy Younger)

boiler made as they swung back and forth—he would make wide detours to avoid them," remembered one local woman.

"Irvine's Whales were where Buchanan Street is now. They were roundabouts with a whale's head and tail each seating ten or twelve and they went up and down as well as round," said Tom Carmichael. "The Joywheel was like a great big saucer, where you sat in the middle and it spun round until it gradually threw them to the edge, but you never heard any complaints. White's Steam Yachts were boats with an engine in the middle which drove them round. Some of the stalls were lit with flare lamps which hung up, with an open white flame like a blowlamp on them."

Many show families can trace their rides and equipment back through generations. "The White family had elaborate rides from about 1900 or before," said Joe Richard White. "John White had his Scenic Gondolas around 1895 and George White had his Venetian Gondolas in 1905, which travelled by rail or by his steam engine *Star of Bon Accord*. My family had the Razzle Dazzle (or Whirling the Whirl) about 1925. It had an organ on the front of the ride to draw crowds of people, and the loudspeakers faced inwards to let the passengers get the most benefit of the music. White's had the first Rotor in Scotland, which came to the Kelvin Hall in Glasgow in 1950.

"My brother and sister and myself branched out separately in the 1970s, and we travel as JR White's Amusements. My brother is William White and Sons, and my sister is settled and out of the business. I started off with the bikes, the electric Speedway, and then I had the Concorde Flyer which I brought to Kirkcaldy brand new in 1978."

The Big Wheel made its first appearance at the 1959 Market, when the 40 foot high amusement was made in France and brought by road from

Dick's electric Chair o' planes in the early 1900s.
(William Dalgleish)

London. William Hunter, the then market superintendent, said at the time: "As far as I can trace, it is the first time since the Market was instituted that such an amusement has been featured. In addition, we will have the Big Wheel's 'baby brother', an 18 ft high version which is being brought from Wales, with caged-in carriages for the safety of children." Locals found it had a beneficial side-effect which the manufacturers hadn't thought of: "In the morning you went looking underneath for money or anything else that might have fallen out of folks' pockets."

"The Rib Tickler was like a big swing with canvas webbing round it," said a local woman, remembering the Market in the 1950s. "You were sitting in two rows on each side facing each other, maybe about eight on each row. The men started to turn the outside casing, which was all painted but it was only canvas so the light came through. They spun the outside, the walls were moving and you swung up and down so it made you feel disorientated and a bit sick."

Favourites included the Chair o' planes for adults and children, which swung out over the sea wall for an extra thrill, Dodgems, the Ghost Train ("it had spiders, skeletons and strings trailing over your face, it was horrible"), and the perennial delight of the Waltzers.

"The Waltzers were a must," said Dryna Innes, remembering her teenage years in the 1960s. "You went on with your pal, and the two of you got into the carriage and the chap would come and throw on the metal bar for you to hold on to, as a safety measure. They always seemed to be good looking guys, and he would birl you round before the ride had started. If it was young girls on their own, these guys would come round and jump on the edge of your carriage and just keep on birling you. If you really wanted a fantastic ride, you would throw out the bar so there was nothing to hold on to. When you went with your boyfriend, you always got a cuddle with his arm round to protect you. If you were with a boy on the Waltzers, the young guys left you alone; but if it was two or four girls they got extra attention, and they birled you one way and then another so you just screamed and screamed! That was the great thing about the Waltzers, you could always have a good scream.

"The Steamboats were two square boxes and the base was made of metal or whatever, but the top was a heavy rope. There weren't any seats, and you all stood up and laced your arms through the rope to keep you steady when it went up and down and got higher. The Dive Bombers were shaped like two bombs with four people in each, and they went up and down and then turned right over. The Meteorite had individual cages where you stood up and they shut you in, and the whole thing spun round and round and then tipped up on its side."

Specialist firms in the UK and many continental countries such as Italy, Spain, France, Germany and Holland design and assemble rides and attractions. One long established (though now no longer in business) firm in Scotland was Maxwell's of Musselburgh which made fairground rides, with their particular speciality being the Waltzer. One of their rides, the

Part of the scene at the 1985 Market by day . . . (A Crawford)

. . . and taken from exactly the same spot at night. (A Crawford)

The Ghostbuster and Dan Taylor's Waltzer sat opposite side-stalls and living wagons in 1985.
(Nancy Brodie)

A general view of the 1979 Market
(Nancy Brodie)

The Pirate Ship and Telstar were two attractions in 1991.
(Nancy Brodie)

Richard and Mary McGillvary celebrated their Golden Wedding at the 1999 Market.
(Mr and Mrs McGillvary)

Pink sugar hearts, the traditional Market sweets, were still on sale in the 1950s.
(Fife Council Museums: Kirkcaldy Museum and Art Gallery)

The Meteorite made its first
visit to the Market in 1964
when rides were sixpence
and a shilling . . .
(Fife Council Libraries)

. . . with the Dive Bombers
beside it.

(D Bell)

An early set of Dive Bombers with the
Big Wheel in the background.
(Fife Council Libraries)

Speedway, appeared at the 1960 Market—but only just in time, according to the local paper of the day. "A few hours before the Market was due to open, a squad of workmen were frantically busy erecting a new motor bike Speedway, from the broad front stairway of which Provost Gourlay was to perform the opening ceremony," said the *Fife Free Press* report. "The Speedway had been promised for the end of March, but for some reason it had been delayed. Almost before the last coat of paint was dry, it was rushed to Kirkcaldy from the works in Musselburgh and was bolted together in the space of a few hours."

Maxwell's also built a set of hobby horses to an American patent—and decorated with stars and stripes—which in 1964 was said to be the first set of horses ever built in Scotland. The firm also built up the bodies of lorries for the showmen, and during the winter months they varnished and repaired the paintwork on the rides ready for the new season. Many rides are still built in Britain, and one of the most popular is the Sizzler Twist which first appeared in the 1980s and is now built under licence by various firms. Many of today's sophisticated, hi-tech rides come from all over Europe, with Top Buzz, Chaos and Superspin made by KMG in Holland, Wild Mouse made by Reverchon in France, and the sky-high Bomber and the Eclipse (which arrived on site just in time for the opening of the 2003 Market) made in Italy.

A set of modern Gallopers in the 1980s when fibreglass had replaced hand-carved wood.
(Fife Council Museums: Kirkcaldy Museum and Art Gallery)

The rides themselves—and the lorries which transport them—hold a particular fascination for members of the Fairground Association of Great Britain which started up in 1978. Graham Downie, who has been chairman of the association since its inception, explained that the idea to form the group was born in Kirkcaldy. "I was here for the Links Market and started talking to another fairground enthusiast, Pete Tei, and we decided it would be good to start some kind of club which would bring us all altogether to share our interest. Although it covers the whole of the UK, you could say that it really started here in Fife. The Fairground Association provides a focal point where like-minded people can share their views and interests, encourage the wellbeing of fairs and fairgrounds and the study of the history of fairgrounds, and to support the needs of the showmen.

"We produce our own magazine, the *Fairground Mercury*, and have a programme of events during the course of the year throughout the country. These include exhibitions where members display the models they have made of fairground rides, photographs and ephemera. We have held two in Kirkcaldy so far which have drawn a great deal of interest.

White's Chair o' planes still kept the traditional format in the 1970s ... (David Springthorpe)

... and they drew the crowds in the 2003 Market (Andrew Beveridge, Fife Council)

The original Wilmot's Gallopers still came to the Market in 1978. Each horse was named and there was one black horse in the line-up.
(Arnot Muir)

The sophisticated Eclipse made its first appearance at the 2003 Market.
(Andrew Beveridge, Fife Council)

The two giant Big Wheels are pictured almost side by side at the 1997 Market.
(David Springthorpe)

Charlotte Evans' living wagon parked on the Prom around 1973 with its lace curtains, gilt decoration and red and white awning to keep the sun off the paintwork.
(Arnot Muir)

"Our biggest achievement in our first quarter-century has been to support the establishment of the National Fairground Archive at Sheffield University. It collects and holds photographs, documents, memorabilia and recollections so that these important archives are in safe keeping for posterity."

Another keen member is Alan Ingram, who explained that there were different specialist interests within the Association. "Personally, I'm interested in the whole concept of the fairground, the here-today, gone-tomorrow, the transitory nature of the thing. It's the fact that the fair comes and creates a very different environment to the usual ordinary place—and then it disappears," he said.

"A lot of people got interested because of the lorries. In the 1950s and 1960s, showmen used old buses and converted them, painted out the windows, cut out back doors and doors on the roof to hold the equipment. You could see and hear the lorries coming a mile off: even if you half closed your eyes, you could recognise them as fairground transport. Now it's road haulage with the rides just folding down, and you have to look twice before you realise it's a fairground lorry.

"There has always been something new coming along. I suppose you've got at the back of your mind that it can't be improved or developed any further, but it hasn't happened yet: it continues to amaze us that they're moving on and on and on. There were always novelty rides, like the Dive Bombers, and they moved on to become the 'big hitters'. They're the high-tech rides like the Bomber, Eclipse, Wild Mouse, the ones which are essentially big machines and which have a spectacular presence in all the big fairs including the Links Market.

"The showmen have always moved with the times. The thrill rides are a trend in themselves because now teenagers like to be scared half to death; but in the 1940s and 1950s when people were developing novelty rides, some didn't succeed because they were too frightening for the customers of the day. In the late 1960s with the space race and the

General view of the site, including the living wagons, looking towards the bus garages by day . . .
(Don Swanson)

. . . and after dark, looking towards Ravenscraig flats, illuminated by hundreds of lights.
(Don Swanson)

moon landings, they brought in the Astronaut, the Moon Rocket came back, and the Lunar Jet. Round about the 1970s, every Waltzer became a Disco Waltzer because discos had just come in, and that lasted for about ten years and then there was the Breakdance Waltzer. The prizes move on too to attract what people want, silver scooters or whatever the current trend is. Even the art work uses imagery to subliminally attract people to the rides—if you look closely at the big airbrushed figures on modern rides you can see faces which look like celebrities—it all draws people in."

One of the members of the Fairground Association was so enthusiastic that he ran away from school to join the travelling fair. "The big fair came to Hamilton where I stayed, and when I was a youngster I used to go down and help out," said Jim Hemphill. "When I was 14, I ran away from the school— I had about six months to go before I left—to work with the Big Wheel. They wrote a letter to my headmaster saying I was a good wee worker, and he wrote back saying 'He's as well with you because he was never at the school anyway.'

"I worked mainly for John Codona and came to Kirkcaldy with his Waltzer for the first time in 1972 when I was 16. I set it up, painted all the platforms and tidied up what was needing done, did the lights and the music, and went under the machine to check that everything was all right ready for the opening. I have my HGV licence which was a help. Everyone used to meet up at the Links Bar, all the lads from the different firms.

Jimmy Graham is pictured at the wheel of a restored traction engine.
(Fife Council Museums: Kirkcaldy Museum and Art Gallery)

"It was really something to watch the lorries pull on, especially when the living wagons were there too and it was a race to get into your own wee space—it used to be quite a thing to watch. It was a privilege to be taken on by the showmen and I made sure that I was reliable and didn't disappear off the site.

"It's a hard way of living, the showmen's life. The Codona family were always famous for their painted art work which they kept immaculate. They would rub it down with steel wool, and touch up any paintwork that had faded—there was a real art in it. Even if there was just a wee bit flaked off inside the line, that would all be restored and by the time they had finished it and revarnished it, it looked like new."

Arnot Muir, who has always taken more than a passing interest in the showmen's world, is another of the early members of the Fairground Association. His fascination for photographing the fairground lorries and rides led to regular reports and pictures in the *World's Fair* for which he was Scottish correspondent for more than 30 years.

"Traction engines were my first interest from when I was a wee boy," he said. "The restored ones

Thomas Newton's 1949 ERF lorry pictured at the 1978 Market.
(David Springthorpe)

A beautifully restored traction engine was brought to pull Graham's Golden Gallopers in 1988.
(Nancy Brodie)

Joseph R White's Atkinson lorry stands beside the sea wall at the 1979 Market.
(David Springthorpe)

Frank Codona's
Razzle Dazzle at the
1978 Market.
(David Springthorpe)

Mr and Mrs Dawson
are pictured with
their eleven children
and Bruce the family
dog in the early
1900s. In her younger
days, Mrs Dawson
walked tightrope
across Bristol
suspension bridge.
(Elizabeth Carter)

The late Joe Richard
White (back, third
right) and his wife
Emma on the occasion
of their 40th wedding
anniversary along
with their family.
(Joe Richard White)

you see today are all brightly painted in gold and red and blue with polished brasses, but they were never like that in their working lives. They worked seven days a week, pulling down the rides and then they pulled everything to the new venue and often had to go back again for a second load. They were used to build up again and then they provided the power to run the rides.

"I remember the Gallopers of course, and I seem to recall the attendant tapping with a coin on the side of the steam organ in time to the music. The rides in the old days were mainly Dodgems, Waltzers and Speedways. I remember Dan Taylor who had the Whip and the Dodgems; he had a house in Glasswork Street in Kirkcaldy where the family lived in the winter. He used to advertise his rides with placards saying 'Support your local man', which people did."

In the 1970s Arnot Muir started to go down to the Prom on the Sunday morning with his camera to record the lorries coming in and the rides being built up. "In the early days, the showmen didn't like that, they thought you were somebody official snooping around, but that's all changed now," he said. "In those days the lorries really looked like showmen's lorries; they were custom built to suit the different rides, so you could see one coming and knew it was a Waltzer or whatever. The lorries themselves were beautifully lettered with the showmen's names on them. Now they're all built on platforms or low loaders and look just the same on the road."

Expectations of enjoyment have changed over the years. "People used to come along as a family with nice gentle rides for the kids," said one showman. "Teenagers now don't want that, they want white-knuckle rides which frighten the life out of them. Showmen have to keep coming up with new and different ideas to please the public. Show people have been inventing something new to amuse and entertain people for a long time now, and I'm sure that will continue in the future."

Dan Taylor's Waltzer in 1958. A Kirkcaldy man, he put 'Support your local man' on his posters and people responded well.
(National Fairground Archive)

Chapter 6
Showmen remember

"When we were at the Links Market when I was young, they used to give all the kids a sort of Sunday School picnic in the church hall on the Links, and we all got buns. That was on the first Wednesday, before the days when they had the official opening," said Harriet Hanley, whose family have attended the Market for generations. "When we were just wee girls, my cousin Henrietta and me went and played on the sands and we walked along and came to a beach beside the Tiel Burn. When the tide comes in you can't get back over it, so we were sitting there waiting for the tide to go out so we could go back, and we saw all these lights on the beach—they were searching for us. We weren't allowed out for three days afterwards.

"My father had a roll the pennies stall, we call them wheel 'em ins, a round stall with the tables tapering down to the centre. My father got 10 ft of ground in Kirkcaldy when he got married, next year he got another two foot and the next year, another two foot. Our stall was right beside one of the houses on the Prom, and in those days we used to have to pull down the roll the penny stall on the Saturday night, so the lady in the house beside us could see through her window on the Sunday. Sunday used to be a great day in Scotland.

"On Sunday morning, all the children went round the caravans and got our Sunday money— mostly we got a wooden threepenny. You got dressed up in your best—we called it our Kirkcaldy flash!" It's more than likely that Harriet was one of the girls whose dresses Myra Bell admired so much when she looked over at the caravans from her home in Links Street.

Many show people got married in Kirkcaldy during the time of the Links Market; some were born in Fife. "Four of our family were born in wagons—there were no doctors, all our aunties or the older women would deliver the babies,"

Annunziata (Nancy) Paris with her grandson Philip in front of their living wagon around 1927.
(Philip Paris)

The showmen's living wagons were an attraction in themselves to local people. Lizzie Dick holds new baby Teenie, with her elder daughter Cissie seated in the foreground and the girls' young aunt, Nancy Clark, sitting beside the baby.
(William Dalgleish)

Harriet Hanley said. "We were never christened in the same place as we were born, because by that time we would have moved on to the next place. When we were children and heard someone was going to have their baby, we used to sit outside the wagon waiting to see what was going to happen." Another show-woman produced her aunt's birth certificate, dated 1877, with "Place of birth: in a wagon in High Street, Glasgow" and "Father's occupation: acrobat".

"I often heard the story that when my mother was being born in the family wagon when they were in Blairgowrie, my grandfather went to get the nurse to give my grandmother a hand at the birth," said one man. "The nurse refused to come because she thought she was going to some dirty old place. So my grandfather went and spoke to the bank manager and he told the nurse to come; of course when she saw inside the wagon it was spotless with all the ornaments and everything. She apologised, and later on they became friends, my grandmother and the nurse."

Everyone remembered the treats for the show children. "People would come round from the Mission and they used to invite us up for tea when you took your own cup," said one man. And everyone remembered Kirkcaldy's social life. "We all used to go to the Burma dance hall on the Prom, we couldn't get enough of it. They played *In the Mood*, and my mother and I used to go there," said one show-woman.

"I remember away back, wanting to hurry up to get to Kirkcaldy to get to the dancing at the Burma, I loved it there. We pulled in on the Sunday and I used to go to the Burma about four times that week," said Lilian White. "That was where I learned to dance, and of course there were proper bands then. We had our own Showmen's Dance on the Thursday night there for two or three years, after we closed down, but that's all stopped now. Years later they changed it to a Sunday night for the younger kids."

Frances and Henrietta Knowles have more direct local connections with Kirkcaldy than most show people. "My mother belonged Kirkcaldy and her grandfather, James McKinnon, was the first Labour councillor in Kirkcaldy," Frances said. "Her uncle married a woman who was in this business and when he was in the Army, my Mammy went to help her and that's how she met my Daddy, when he came to the Links Market. There's not very many people would choose this as a lifestyle unless they were born into it. Although my Mammy was a local, this was her life and she loved it. She sat there at the stall on the day she died, she was just six months off being ninety."

Her sister Henrietta said: "My Daddy used to tell us that when he was young, it was horses that moved them from place to place. When they got to the Links, my Daddy had to go with the horses to a farm away out past Dysart that used to let them graze their horses, and walk back.

"We think we've got it hard, but they went to the same fairs that we go to now with steam engines. They had to get up at four in the morning to get the fires lit to get the steam up for us to go away about seven. Our steam engine pulled two trucks and a caravan at the back of them, and a binco box which was a chest all lined with cedar wood with a lovely smell, to carry the binco lights for the stall. Then there was a trailer called a dandy at the back of that to carry the water—though they said our engine couldn't pass a river

A studio photograph, complete with giant beer bottle, at a showmen's outing in the 1950s. Billy Codona is pictured on the right in the back row with Harry Paris next to him.
(Philip Paris)

This wonderfully atmospheric photograph taken in 1913 shows the Dick family on the road near Blairgowrie. The horse-drawn wooden Molycroft wagon is followed by a trailer with Swingboats, and behind that is the 'big wagon' which doubled up as a shooting stall with a chip cart bringing up the rear. The photograph, which was taken by Alick Dick includes Lizzie Dick and her sister-in-law Barbara, Bob Dick (standing on the grass), Davie Clark beside the Swingboats, Willie Clark and one of their workers, Wee Starry, at the chipper, as well as the horses, Bobby and Sausage, with Henry Dick at the front.
(William Dalgleish)

without needing to fill up. My Mammy used to make up a wee basket and we would sit outside and have a wee picnic at the side of the road while they filled up with water. The roads were no way like they are now, they were quiet, you were lucky if you saw a horse and cart on the road.

"The wagon was painted outside and inside there was a top and bottom bed, Mammy and Daddy in the top and we were in the bottom. There was a table, lockers there and there, a wee narrow cupboard, and when the beds were pulled out they came right over the locker. There was a lot of brass, and we had to do the brasses every day."

Lilian White remembered polishing the brasses too. "My mother had all the ornaments and brasses—the older people liked that, they're not seen so much now. She liked Dresden figures and her wee bits of Crown Derby and I used to wash them all with my father's shaving brush! I don't really like ornaments now, I washed so many when I was young. We had lace curtains which I like myself; we had frilly lace curtains which we used to change every month. I was brought up to wash and polish, that was the one thing my mother taught me, how to clean.

"My own family name was Newton, and I was born in a wagon on the Braes in Saltcoats. My mother had three of us in a wagon; the women didn't go to maternity hospitals as they do now. It was a tiny wee wagon, a Molycroft, about 12 foot long with steps at the front, but there was a place for everything and everything was always in its place. By the time my sister was born ten years later, my parents had a bigger caravan which they had made for them. My sister and I slept in the top beds which slid out, my brother was in the bottom bed and our parents were in the bedroom.

"When we came to Kirkcaldy when I was a child, there were none of these new houses on the Prom and the flats weren't built. I remember going

The White family at the Golden Wedding celebrations of Joseph and Mary Ellen White in 1952.
(Joe Richard White)

through a vennel round to the wee home bakery in Links Street and getting lovely cakes and scones."

The rides and attractions drew not only visitors to the Market but the showmen's families themselves. "When we were children, we all looked forward to going to the Links Market and we always went to see the circuses," said show-woman Elizabeth Carter. "I remember there used to be two Pinder circuses up in the Basin car park, near where my family's site was. One had Tommy Pinder who was the lion tamer, an excellent performance which children don't see now—to me, a circus is not a circus without animals.

"There was also Miss Amelia and Miss Elizabeth Pinder who did tightrope, horseback riding and trapeze. They used to dance in front of the circus, as an attraction to draw people in, an entertainment before they went into the circus—they were like Dresden figures. The circuses gave a free performance on the outside before people went in."

Elizabeth Pinder and her younger sister Amelia started coming to Kirkcaldy when they were children, when their grandmother had one of the circuses. Along with Amelia's husband Harry, better known as Koko the Clown, they were versatile entertainers with each one proficient in several acts. One of Koko's routines included performing dogs with miniature cars and a carriage, something which would perhaps not be acceptable to public taste today. "But all the dogs were strays and mongrels taken in by Harry and humanely trained," said nephew Edwin Pinder. "They were family pets and the showmen's livelihood. It came naturally to them and it was in our interests to treat them well."

The Pinder sisters continued coming to Kirkcaldy until they were in their eighties, long after the circus had finished. They were determined to carry on in the business as long as they could, bringing a collection of pets and small animals, and a magic mirror sideshow. One show-woman said: "I always remember Lizzie Pinder saying 'Keep right on to the end of the road, that's what Harry Lauder said!'"

When they eventually retired in the late 1980s and settled in Glasgow, Elizabeth Pinder spoke about the early days of the family circus. "I was taught by my father, uncles and aunties, and we all took after the tradition. I was what we called an all-rounder, I would do a single act on my own or a double act with my sister. One man said to me once when I was performing, balancing on the wire, 'I wish I had as good a balance in the bank.' My grandmother, who owned the circus then, bought our elephant in Germany. He was a lovely wee elephant but he got very big, and I performed with him with my father. People used to say in Leith if someone was clumsy, 'Lift your feet, you're like Pinder's elephant.' I enjoyed going to the different places and meeting people who recognised us. "

Her sister Amelia Salvona also remembered days gone by. "I started performing when I was about 14. The first thing I really did in public was juggle, my sister and brother and me, we all did a juggling act. Then about the next year I learned to do the horse riding—later on I did the ballerina but it was only as you came on a bit that you did the fancy things. My brothers were horse riders, and you just went and jumped on and off the horse and did little things until you could do it on your own. I was small and I wasn't heavy, and my dad thought, well if you look the part, it is the part, so that's how I got the job. Lizzie was a little heavier, so she was the wire walker.

"My father, he was the circus man. He could be the ringmaster, he was

the lion tamer, he was the elephant man—he went in with the elephant, because they get to know just one person so nobody else can take it in that ring and show it. It was a very big elephant, a male, it was quite good and it could pull one of the caravans along the road. But I never took to elephants, and when I go and see a circus now I don't go near the elephants. I don't know what it was, maybe because it was big and I was small.

"I didn't have a stage name, they called me Amelia, but when I did the horse riding I was the Ballerina or the Lady Equestrian, and Lizzie, she was called the Lady Wire Walker. My husband Harry—they called him Koko—came from a circus family himself. We got married when I was about 24, and he was there all his life with us and ran the circus. We liked the horses and ponies, monkeys and dogs. We had a little pony and it used to pick the red hankie out of one box and the white hankie out of the other—my husband would switch them round but the pony still knew which it was. People always remembered that and they would say 'You were the one with the pony.' When my oldest daughter came into the circus we called her Tandalayo the human fly, because she walked upside down—she walked the loops with her toes and hung upside down.

"When my husband died, we sold the circus, and we went on to have side shows like a Genie in the Bottle and the Magic Mirrors, and we opened up a Mini-zoo. There wasn't such a lot of work in that. We travelled them—oh, it must have been for 20 years—and we never missed Kirkcaldy."

Their great-nephew Edwin Pinder said: "The family circus started up in 1861. For the last five or six generations, the eldest son of each generation has always called Edwin Ord Pinder, so myself and my son are both called that. Although we have changed from circuses to suit the public taste, we still keep a run of fairs and follow the same circuit as my great-grandfather did. Now we have Funhouses, but we still have my great-aunts' Magic Mirror show and Mini-zoo which we keep for sentimental reasons and sometimes put them on as exhibitions."

Amelia Pinder on horseback with her husband Koko. (Edwin Pinder)

Edwin Pinder in his full clown make-up.
(Edwin Pinder)

Showmen have always had to be versatile and able to turn their hands to anything needing done on the fairground. "He's got to be an electrician, an engineer, a joiner and a mechanic," said one man. "He has to be a bit of everything, a jack of all trades, that's a proper showman."

Fifer William Dalgleish from Lochore, who comes from two lines of show families, Clark and Dick, and who is the first generation of his family to come out of the fairground business, agreed. "There wasn't a thing my grandfather Bob Dick couldn't put his hand to, like all showmen. He painted all the rides and stalls himself, he was a fine painter and I still have all his brushes and the gold leaf he used for the signs," he said. "He had premises at the Port Brae in Kirkcaldy where they spent the winter; he was painting one of the rides in his yard there and two men who had a big painters' business in the town were standing watching him. They asked him how long it had taken him to learn sign-writing—in these days you had to serve a seven-year apprenticeship—and they could hardly believe him when he said he had just picked it up by watching other men painting.

"My mother Teenie Dick and her sister Cissie both went to school in Kirkcaldy, in Milton Road, and went to Sunday School at St James Church at the Port Brae. Auntie Cissie left school when she was 14 so my mother left too, she said 'If she's left the school, so have I.' They would be up working with my grandfather, it was a hard life. They used to push the kids' ride round on a track and they took the money for the family Chair o' planes, which had a steam organ in the middle of it, and a Swingboat.

"His father, my great-grandfather, used to buy a whole railway wagon load of coconuts from Covent Garden in the 1900s and bring it up to the Market—they called him the Coconut King. My great grandparents, Geordie and Celie Clark, had chippers with coal fires to cook the chips over. They came to Kirkcaldy every year, and that would be where their daughter Lizzie met and married Bob Dick, my grandfather. He had Chair o' planes and a shooter or shooting gallery. My grandmother opened up the shooting gallery at the Port Brae when the men were all away at the First War. I still have her letter telling my grandfather that when she was left in Kirkcaldy with the

two bairns, she took one of the rifles into the caravan with her for protection. He was later invalided out of the Army and came back to the business.

"A couple of years ago, when my Auntie Cissie was 90, we took her away for a long weekend and revisited all the sites down the west coast where they used to go with the shows. The show people were in the exact places where they used to go, and at one place we were invited into one of the wagons and the man took his cap off to her. She still had all her faculties, and could remember all the places and say 'This is where the wheel came off the traction engine.' It was good that she could see all the old routes again before she died.

"Her father used to have a traction engine and when he was driving it, he wouldn't move for anyone. He went all over the country in it, and he was the first man to take a traction engine down the Kintyre peninsula to Campbeltown. There weren't many cars on the roads then, but if he met anyone coming the other way, he wouldn't pull over to the side because the engine would have toppled over. When he was going up hills, my mother and my aunt had to go to the back and put coconut sacks under the wheels to stop them slipping. Auntie Cissie was very small, and when the boiler of the traction engine was being repaired, they put her inside it to help clean it out.

"My mother met my father, who was an electrician in the pit, and when they got married in 1937 she left the fairground business. When I was 15, I wanted to go back into the shows, but my grandfather wouldn't let me—he said it was too hard a life."

Minnie Paris, Philip's mother, comes from a very well known showground family. "My father was Billy Codona, and he had a big set of Dragons which he took to the Links Market. The Dragons were a mechanical ride that the people sat on, a lot of scarlet and gold, and it was painted to look like scenery with a bit of a hill on it. Even the show people used to walk up specially to see his Dragons.

"He had his own traction engine, the *Carry On*, and when I was a kid the family had three engines,

Clark's 'chipper' in the 1900s with Kate Clark, Davie and Willie Clark. The chips were cooked in the coal-fired stove on the left of the cart. Willie later took the horse-drawn chipper to Thornton Games where it went on fire and he came back only with the horse. The hand-painted lettering on The Royal includes Clark on the canopy with Chipped Potatoes at the front.

(William Dalgleish)

Teenie Dick (right), who later married Andrew Dalgleish and left the fairground business, her sister Cissie (later Goodwin) and (front) Davie Clark around 1925.

(William Dalgleish)

Challenger, Rising Star, and *Dorothy.* The engine led three loads, then the caravan, then another load, then the dandy—though we sometimes used the water in it for washing. There was a special box for the binco lights, they were flare lamps as far as I can remember, which were used for lighting up a lot of equipment.

"I don't remember my grandfather, William Codona Snr as I was only five when he died, but they used to travel with the shows in the summer. My Dad had three brothers and three sisters, they had the firm Codona Brothers—himself, Frankie and then Nathaniel. They were all together at one time and then after World War I the brothers all split up and went their own way.

"I was born in a wagon, beside Bellahouston Park in Glasgow, near the Rangers pitch. It was more like a rail wagon, they had wagons that were lower because they were built to go on a rail track. My mother had six children, but as the years went on, the boys got places of their own. They would have a wee wagon, a little place inside the lorry just past the cab with a bit partitioned off and bunk beds which pulled out—you can still see some of them.

"We had a wooden Molycroft caravan, which had the middle part of the roof raised up with wee windows; half of it was for living in and half was for packing. They painted the wooden roof with a mixture of white lead and linseed oil, for waterproofing. In the winter they put calico on top, the stuff they made sails and that from. They would paint it again and maybe put a bit of green paint in. I remember hearing someone saying: 'They show folk must be awful cold with just that canvas on top'—they didn't realise there was wood underneath!

"During the war there were some small 'holiday-at-home' fairs to keep people's spirits up. We had blackout covers and special dim lights, but they

Billy Codona, founder of William Codona and Sons Ltd, around 1940.
(Philip Paris)

Frank Codona's *Carry On* engine in 1938.
(National Fairground Archive)

weren't a success. All the men were away in the Army so it was just the women and some of the old men. I helped out, I did the lifting of the money and helped to scrub and clean and all that, but my Dad never let us pack up the rides. With stalls it's a different thing, but if it's machines, it's a man's job.

"I remember some of the prizes—we call them 'swag'—that we used to give out before the war, some of these things like hand-cut tumblers, coloured glass, wee dishes, butter plates—you see them in antique shops now. Some of the stalls had beautiful cut glass stuff on them or tea sets. At the shooters, that's the shooting galleries, you had to score 21 to get a prize. If you scored 24, that was like four bull's-eyes, you got the pick of the stall and the tea sets would be the top prize."

Until the advent of Calor gas, heating in most of the wagons was by Hostess stove, a small coal burning stove which also had cooking facilities. "They were finished in cream coloured enamel," recalled Frances Knowles, "but one of the show women, we called her Auntie Subie, was fanatical about painting everything and one day she painted her Hostess stove. It was fine until she lit it and then the smell of the paint was awful.

"She was a real character, she used to have an old wireless with batteries in it and she asked

Adverts in *The World's Fair* in 1927 for goldfish, tortoises, and side-stall prizes.

someone to take it to get charged up; he was swinging it and she said 'Don't swing it like that, you'll mix up all my stations!' She called us all 'daughter', and she would say to me 'Daughter, get me a fish supper' and she would give me threepence which wasn't nearly enough. I had to run all the way round the fairground to get my Daddy to give me more money."

Showmen's living wagons now are comfortable, luxurious and well-planned homes with as many (or more) labour saving devices as any static accommodation. "A caravan can be 8'6" wide when it's on the road but 12 foot when it's static," explained Philip Paris. "You pull on the side walls and they slide out to give you more room—with the new ones you just press a button. But caravans like that are becoming less and less popular with showmen, particularly now that the cost of fuel is astronomical. I'd like to have a permanent site of my own with a permanent chalet and somewhere to park all the equipment on, with a smaller caravan to travel in over the summer."

The close-knit community of showmen's families was commented on by Alfred Codona when he was interviewed in the 1960s. "The chances are that all the showmen in the Scottish section are related in some way to each other, it's the way it is. I suppose it's the life we lead, always on the move, always living in such close community with other fairground people. When a man wants to look for a wife, he naturally looks for somebody who understands his business and who can take such an important part in running it with him. That means somebody who is already with the fairs and who has probably grown up in it too."

His views were echoed by Philip Paris more than forty years later. "Most show families that I know now can trace back their ancestry in this business for a hundred years or more. They used to be in travelling theatre, the 'penny geggies', I believe that's how they started, doing these sort of shows in conjunction with fairs or galas and eventually came into the business. My great-grandfather on my father's side was an Italian immigrant, they had a chip cart and ice cream, and they must have expanded from that. My wife is a Wilmot, my uncles are Codonas, my mother's mother was a Broughton, all well known Scottish show family names. You're all related somehow or other, it's a long established way of life.

"My grandmother Agnes Smith lost both her parents when she and her brother Hugh were quite young. She and her brother travelled with the Wilmots as part of the family, and she would help out with cooking and cleaning. She was with the Wilmots until she married my grandfather Harry Paris, who had the coconut 'sheets' or coconut shy. After she was married, they took in her younger sister Louise, our Auntie Louie, who was the youngest of the family and she lived with my grandmother and grandfather. It was quite common in those days for young people to travel round with their relations and it meant that they could lend a hand with looking after the younger children. If they had big families, they would sometimes have another caravan used as a kitchen wagon drawn up beside the living wagon, to give extra space for cooking and eating.

"Some of the side stalls are put up by the women who run them, if it's not too big a job. What tends to happen is that your children help you in the stalls because you can't afford to employ working men for extra labour. Once it's all set up, the family members usually work together in operating and 'lifting' or collecting the fares.

"This business is changing; for instance, travelling on motorways means you can't stop to meet up with other showmen as easily as you used to. But I still say that if you're pulled in at the side of the road, any showman passing you will toot their horn and you put your thumb up to tell him you're all right, it's always been that way."

Harry Paris (left) in the 1950s with a Molycroft wagon in the background.
(Philip Paris)

Harriet Hanley agreed that the pace of modern life affected their business. "In the old days, if anyone broke down on the way somewhere, you would see a line of show people at the side of the road. All the women used to stand out and have a talk, but now there's no time. We used to be able to travel, stop at the side of the road and have our dinner, but you can't do that today on the motorways, you've got to get there in one day."

Another showman remembered that when he was a boy in the 1920s, all the equipment was hauled around by horses. "That wasn't too easy at all," he said. "I would often have to walk at the back of the caravan because my little bit of extra

Agnes Paris (grandmother of Philip Paris) is pictured on the right with (from left) Louise, Sarah, Hugh and Charlotte Smith.
(Philip Paris)

A programme from the first Scotland versus England showmen's football match organised by the Showmen's Social Association of Great Britain in 1953.
(Philip Paris)

weight would have been just too much. Sometimes that meant I had to trail behind the caravan for many miles."

"It's a very hard life which sometimes people don't understand, but it's a good clean-living entertaining one," said Elizabeth Carter. "My family have been in the business all their lives, and their family before them, and I'm very proud to say I am a show-woman."

Most showmen learned to drive at a tender age. "Before the Second War my grandfather bought a bus from Forrester's, took the cab off the chassis, and rebuilt it to make a living wagon with a wee coal stove," said William Dalgleish. "When he got his first lorry, he had an hour to learn how to drive it and then he was off."

Joe Richard White, who was born in the Govan area of Glasgow in 1932, had the same introduction to driving. "I learned to drive at 14, and if you were hanging around, your father stuck you on a lorry and you just got on with it. Mind you there wasn't much traffic on the roads then, not like it is now, " he said. "My grandfather started off with horses and a horse-drawn caravan, moved up to traction engines and then to motors, that's how it worked. You were just brought up to do all the things needed in the fairground business.

"When I started out, they were doing away with the traction engines and the wagons were

A showmen's football team in the 1930s. The picture includes 'Smudger' Smith, Bobby Horne (in suit), goalkeeper Tommy Paulo, Jacky Wright, Billy Newton and Bob Coady.
(Elizabeth Carter)

Mrs Emma White sits at the paydesk of the Speedway around 1955 when rides cost 3*d*. and 6*d*.
(Joe Richard White)

Molycrofts which are very seldom seen now. They were wooden, and we would wash down the paintwork, clean it all up, put the varnish back on— and then put the canvas covers on to keep the paintwork fresh. We did a lot of work on them that was never seen, but we did it all the same. They were followed on by the 'pan loaf', the flat roofed caravan which still had a row of wee windows for ventilation."

Show people have always been justifiably proud of their strong sense of family, and this is seen particularly in the way that they look after their elderly folk. Wherever possible, the older members of the community travel round the fairs with their children and grandchildren, living in their own wagons which are sited nearby. Few showmen want to retire at 60 or 65 and most prefer to carry on helping out in the family business as long as they are able. Some do 'settle down' by opening static amusement arcades at seaside towns, keeping in the business but without travelling round the country.

The family tradition is also seen in the practice of naming the eldest son after his father; many showmen have two Christian names and are known by them both. "So you get Arthur David Hancock, John Henry Codona, George Robert Hanley. It's just a custom, it's not even to distinguish father from son, because Joe Richard White's father was also called Joe Richard," said Philip Paris. "We don't call an older person by his first name, we say 'Uncle John' or 'Aunt Harriet'. I know I'm getting older when people start calling me 'Uncle Philip'! It's a mark of respect, we were brought up to respect our elders and we bring our children up the same way."

Up until fairly recently, education for showmen's children had little continuity, with youngsters attending school at their winter quarters and then disrupted schooling as they travelled with their families around the country. "I was sent to boarding school when I was five, because my father wanted a better education for me than he had," said Philip Paris, admitting with hindsight that going away from home at such an early age was not easy. "There was a lot of bullying and discrimination, which still continues to a certain extent. The system has been greatly improved and now when children go back to their main school in October, the work that they have done in different schools has been forwarded so that they can carry on from that rather than being given something they have already covered. Now there's a national liaison officer, Valerie Moodie, the wife of a showman, who was given the MBE for her work in this field. If the children are interested and want to get an education, they will get it." Many children of showmen are now at college or university, something which through lack of opportunity would have been a rare achievement a generation or two ago.

Like elderly people in any walk of life, some showmen look back to the 'good old days' with nostalgia. "My mother and my people went for years to the Links Market, it was all happy times when I was a kid—we used to stand in the Basin," said one show-woman. "My mother used to say, you put something away for a rainy day, so when we got nothing on one Saturday, we have to make that do to another Saturday. It was always a happy place, that was when people *was* people. Now people don't understand this business, they think you just stand there and take the money.

The late Joe Richard White (right) at Kirkcaldy in the 1950s.
(Joe Richard White)

"All these new regulations have made things different. I don't mean any harm to the firemen, but if there was a fire, the show people would have put it out before they got here, because we're people who have to be alert. It's

our life, we don't sit on our hands and not look around. We look after our children and check them as much as we can, and warn them what not to do and to have respect for their families."

Joe Richard White recalled that his grandparents were one of the first to have a showmen's wagon that had a pull out section to give extra room. "In the Fifties, the Market often used to be opened on one of our rides, and the family's living wagon was parked just behind it," he said. "Before the days when they had the official lunch, the Provost and the Councillors used to go to the caravan at the back and my grandmother Mary Ellen White would lay out a buffet and a wee drink for them. The wagon had two doors, so they had a system of going in one door and out the other.

"We had four rides at one time but now I've just got the Sizzler Twist, it's a family ride. Our family are married now out of the fairground business, and although my wife and I still go round, now that I'm a bit older I don't do so much, I'm only travelling to keep myself in business. I'm not going to give up—us showmen carry on as working people, we keep on to the end of the road. I have enjoyed every minute of it, and I wouldn't change my life for anyone."

A group of showmen and their families posed for the camera at one of Wilmot's rides in Kirkcaldy around 1900.
(William Dalgleish)

Chapter 7
The Carousel Keeps Turning

Kirkcaldy Links Market means many different things to many people.

Visitors come for a wide variety of reasons. They can be local people who just like to stroll through the fair from end to end, enjoying the spectacle without going on any of the rides or taking part in the sideshows, but joining in the atmosphere with their annual candy floss; or they might be teenagers who gather up their money and think nothing of spending £100 in one weekend on the fastest, scariest rides on the Prom. They can be elderly couples who go mainly out of nostalgia, remembering how it used to be, and recalling romances that began on the Waltzers and either fizzled out like spent fireworks or led to lifelong partnerships; or perhaps parents or grandparents introducing the next generation to the Market, handing out pound coins as if they were going out of fashion and delighting in seeing the familiar sights through new young eyes. They can be fairground enthusiasts whose eyes are on the showmen's lorries and the technicalities of each new ride, appreciating the difficulties of building them up and getting ready in time; or perhaps they are children who are determined to try out as many rides, sideshows, hot dogs and toffee apples as time and money allow.

The showmen come to earn a living, but there's more to it than that. There is some prestige involved in having a stance at the Links Market, which is seen among the showmen as one of the top fairs in Britain as well as the largest one in Scotland. Whatever form their business takes, from a single side-stall to a spectacular new ride, it does better at a good fair. For those who have a brand new ride, especially the first of its kind, Kirkcaldy is an excellent sounding board to see how popular it's going to be; if it's successful so early in the season, it can be taken to other sites with confidence, and whoever has built it will have orders for many more. Many come to keep up the long family tradition, standing on the same piece of ground that their fathers or grandfathers did. Then there is the social side to enjoy, catching up with people they haven't seen for some time; because the majority of Scottish showmen travel within the boundaries of Scotland or just over the Border, they see their English counterparts for a drink and a chat when they meet up at Kirkcaldy.

The Links Market as we know it today bears no resemblance to the early fairs initiated by that first Charter in 1304, just as today's world has nothing in common with those long-ago times. And yet the Market has evolved, grown, altered and kept up with the incalculable number of changes which have taken place over the centuries.

Changes in society, working and social conditions, and our perception of what is entertainment have all played a part in shaping today's Market. It has always reflected the mood of the moment. The good folk of Fife who thought the Cakewalk was the last word in entertainment in the 1920s could never have dreamt of the white-knuckle Roller Coasters, Bungee Jumps and Drop Towers which soared high above the crowds some eighty years later. The flamboyant richness of the rides from the 1890s until just before the First War reflected the grand style which was typical of the late Victorian and Edwardian period. Among the austerity and rationing which followed the Second War, the machines were taken out, dusted off and set in motion to help lift embattled spirits. The post-war reluctance to introduce new, more daring rides was not purely a matter of economics: after years of fighting and upheaval, people wanted the reassurance of familiar, friendly rides, and no-one then needed to be artificially frightened out of their wits when they were slowly and painfully recovering from experiencing the real thing.

Each new advance has been incorporated into advertising, marketing and attractions. When electricity started taking over from steam, for instance, this was advertised as a sure-fire draw: "No steam engines employed—every car driven by electricity." When radio came on the scene, press advertising recognised this with enticements such as "Hello! Hello! Kirkcaldy speaking—Broadcast it, something really new!"; and when television advertising jingles were on everyone's lips, juvenile car rides included slogans such as "Put a Tiger in Your Tank". The 1960s attractions echoed the space race, with new names such as the Satellite and the Moon Rocket, and in the 1970s, the disco era lent its name to many rides. Currently many modern rides are painted differently again, reflecting the club scene and depicting today's stars and celebrities.

Anticipation before the event has always been high, with speculation about what new rides would make their appearance. The latest amplification techniques means that the music is louder than in the days of the majestic steam organs, but it still plays the latest hits just as it did when *Daisy, Daisy, It's a Long Way to Tipperaray*, or *Keep Right on to the End of the Road* were sung with gusto. The old favourites which have been around in some shape or form for generations—Dodgems, Waltzers, Chair o' planes, Helter-skelter and Roundabouts—can still be seen: some with new names, shapes or colours to fit in with today's Market, but still substantially the same.

Political correctness has put paid to performing animals and freak shows; the street traders have gone elsewhere to sell their wares; guardians of product licenses have stopped rides bearing names of Disney characters or TV cartoons; and health and safety issues impose new and more stringent requirements with each year that passes.

Showmen have always provided whatever the public want, and as expectations rise, they have made sure of meeting them. They have always been aware of new trends—and have often in fact been ahead of them. They are fully attuned to the current perception of enjoyment so that they can match it: that, after all, is show business.

Perhaps part of the secret of the Market's enduring success and evolution has been the showmen's skill at recognising the latest trends and incorporating them into the scene, while dispensing with ideas which were yesterday's news.

Local people remember with nostalgia the gentler forms of entertainment of the Thirties and the still unsophisticated rides of the Fifties. In days to come, will today's children and teenagers look back with the same fondness on the high-tech machines of the early twenty-first century?

Down the long years, the shape and form of the Market has evolved and altered to keep up with changing times; through it all, the tradition holds firm. For the show people whose business is also their way of life, and the local people who see the yearly event as part of their heritage, the unique and well-loved Links Market is surely set to continue for many long years to come.

Acknowledgements

The author would like to thank everyone who helped in the research of this book and who gave their time, memories and photographs so generously to help build up a picture of the history of Kirkcaldy Links Market. Special thanks are due to Jim and Myra Bell, D Bell, Andrew Beveridge, Fiona Brodie, Nancy Brodie, Tom Carmichael, Elizabeth Carter, Mark Conroy, A Crawford, the late John Crichton, William Dalgleish, Graham Downie, Fairground Association of Great Britain, Fife Council Museums: Dallas Mechan (Museums Co-ordinator), Janice Crane, Gavin Grant, and Kathryn Shearer; Robert Foster, Sheena Graham, Archie Grieve, John Haggart, Ms Hall, Harriet Hanley, Jim Hemphill, Jayne Horsburgh, Alan Ingram, Dryna Innes, Frances Knowles, Henrietta Knowles, Alex Lafferty, John Litster, Helen Main, Albert Marsh, Brian McCormack, Jacqui McDowall, Richard and Mary McGillvary, Alex McGrow, Arnot Muir, Philip and Hayley Paris, Minnie Paris, the late Elizabeth Pinder, Eddie Pinder, Jane Rodgers, the late Amelia Salvona, Scottish Section of the Showmen's Guild of Great Britain, Peter Saunders, Derry Sinclair, David Springthorpe, Jim Swan, Don Swanson, Dr Vanessa Toulmin and Ian Trowell (National Fairground Archive, Sheffield University), Edith Williamson, Wendy Younger, Joe Richard and Lillian White. Particular thanks are due to the staff of Fife Council Libraries who have been involved with this project from the start, and who have given invaluable support and assistance throughout; particularly David Spalding (Libraries Cultural Services Co-ordinator), Audrey Brown, Sheila Campbell, and Janet Klak. Thanks are also due to all the other people who gave assistance but who preferred to remain anonymous, and to those whose contributions could not be included from lack of space, but whose help in building up the background picture was very much appreciated.

Index